10 Days

to More Confident Public Speaking

Also by The Princeton Language Institute

Grammar 101
Guide to Pronunciation
Roget's 21st Century Thesaurus

Also by Lenny Laskowski

Dynamic Presentation Skills for the Business Professional
No Sweat Presentations: The Painless Way to Successful Speaking

10 Days to More Confident Public Speaking

The Princeton Language Institute
and Lenny Laskowski

Produced by The Philip Lief Group, Inc.

GRAND CENTRAL PUBLISHING

NEW YORK BOSTON

Grand Central Publishing
Hachette Book Group
237 Park Avenue
New York, NY 10017

Visit our Web site at www.HachetteBookGroup.com.

Printed in the United States of America

First Edition: July 2001
10 9

Grand Central Publishing is a division of Hachette Book Group, Inc.
The Grand Central Publishing name and logo is a trademark of Hachette Book Group, Inc.

Library of Congress Cataloging-in-Publication Data
10 days to more confident public speaking/The Philip Lief Group, Inc., the Princeton Language Institute, and Lenny Laskowski.
p. cm.
ISBN 978-0-446-67668-7
1. Public speaking. I. Title: Ten days to more confident public speaking. II. Laskowski, Lenny. III. Philip Lief Group. IV. Princeton Language Institute.

PN4121.A13 2001
808.5'1—dc21 00-043837

Book design by Ralph Fowler
Cover design by Jon Valk

This book is dedicated to my son, Michael, and my daughter, Kelly, for their continued support and encouragement during my journey of helping others become better speakers and presenters and during the writing of this book.

Acknowledgments

Some very good friends and colleagues allowed me to use their material and input. Thank you: Tom Antion, Susan Berkley, Janet Esposito, Kare Anderson, Tony Jeary, Lilly Walters, and Patricia Fripp.

Contents

Introduction

If you poll a group of people and ask them their greatest fear, public speaking usually ranks number one. In fact, in surveys I have conducted with clients at hundreds of seminars and workshops, 67 percent find public speaking difficult. The remaining 33 percent are comfortable with their public speaking skills but feel there is room for improvement. No matter which percentile you fall into, *10 Days to More Confident Public Speaking* will help you assess your speaking skills and learn fast, effective strategies to become a better, more confident public speaker.

Throughout my career as a public speaker, I have identified many reasons why people are not comfortable speaking in front of a group, large or small. Some people are self-conscious about their appearance or voice. Others are afraid they will be laughed at or criticized. Such fears can compromise your effectiveness, preventing you from becoming a more confident public speaker.

Improving your public speaking and communication skills increases your self-confidence, but studies have revealed an additional benefit: Professionals with good communication skills are promoted more often and faster within their job environment. Top company executives polled said that the one essential skill they look for in an employee slated for promotion is the ability to effectively communicate ideas. *10 Days to More Confident Public Speaking* provides you with proven, successful methods to increase your confidence as a public speaker. As a public speaking coach and keynote speaker, I have used these tips and methods to help clients from all over the world enhance their speaking, presentation, and communication skills.

10 Days to More Confident Public Speaking is divided into ten days, each one building on skills learned from prior days. Chapters are sprinkled with "Tips of the Day," "Top Ten Lists," "Lessons from Mom," and "Confidence Builders" as well as practical exercises and strategies. Here is a glimpse of what you will take away with you in the course of your ten-day journey.

- **Day 1:** We begin with tips on how to improve your public speaking skills in every area of your life, from career to personal life to social situations. Along the way you will learn a Lesson from Mom on the importance of practicing and polishing your skills. And you will learn quick tricks about ways to introduce yourself to an audience.
- **Day 2:** The most important skill when preparing a presentation is developing speech content. In this chapter you will learn a five-step approach for devising material for your speech or presentation. Also, you will learn the proper structure of a speech—the introduction, body, and conclusion—and hints for eliminating the visual and verbal clutter in your speeches.
- **Day 3:** This chapter focuses on relating to your audience. We begin with steps to analyze your audience and the importance of preprogram and customized surveys to tailor your presentation to meet your audience's needs. The day also includes a Top Ten List of tips and secrets to keep your audience awake and

energized during your presentations. You will also learn the five types of speeches, from informative to impromptu.

- **Day 4:** You will learn the four most common methods for remembering speech and presentation material and the pros and cons for each. In addition, you will find a resource list of Internet Web sites to help your presentation shine. Day 4 ends with how your speech or presentation location can interfere with or enhance your performance.
- **Day 5:** The crux of Day 5 focuses on gestures and the role they play in your presentations. Also, you will learn five tips about facial expressions and why they are an important part of effective communication. The day ends with on-the-spot advice on what to do when you are asked at the last minute to give a presentation.
- **Day 6:** This chapter focuses on the language and ethics behind speech giving, including guidelines for proper attribution of statistics, research results, and quotes. In the process, you will spend some time looking at excerpts from the top ten influential and memorable speeches in history. Also, you will learn ten ways to incorporate humor in your presentation. Day 6 takes an in-depth look at the first of the five types of speeches you learned in Day 3.
- **Day 7:** Throughout Day 7 you will learn tips and secrets that professional speakers, trainers, and entertainers use when the unexpected happens—from room changes to equipment failure. In addition, you will learn fun icebreaker games to use at a training session or seminar. Day 7 also gives you an example of a ceremonial speech.

- **Day 8:** This chapter discusses a variety of special techniques to help you develop and hone your speaking skills. Day 8 also gives an in-depth review process of videotaping yourself as a way to critique your speech before the big day. Finally, you are given a sample of an after-dinner speech.
- **Day 9:** The focus of this chapter is how to psych yourself up for the big moment. The chapter is sprinkled with tips and strategies to show you how to become your own best coach and the importance of making a checklist. In addition, you will learn the humorous way one presenter prepares himself just before he's introduced. Finally, you will get a glimpse of a persuasive speech and how to deliver bad news or negative results in a speech.
- **Day 10:** This chapter shows you how to end your speech or presentation with a memorable conclusion using five surefire methods. You are also introduced to the most effective way to handle the question and answer period following your speech or presentation and how to deal with hostile questions from audience members. Finally, you are given a sample of the fifth type of speech—the impromptu.

Okay, it's time to get started. Turn to Day 1 and get yourself ready for a journey to the world of more confident public speaking.

10 Days
to More Confident Public Speaking

Day 1

Getting Started

Overcoming Your Fears

For as long as I can remember, I always think back to when I was only five years old. I would spend the day outside either playing in the dirt or building. At the end of the day I would talk my parents' ears off (I assumed they were listening) about what I built or what I was going to build. Little did I realize that my training as an engineer—my first career—was already beginning.

One day in school, somewhere around the turn of the century, my first-grade teacher, Mrs. Collins, asked the class for volunteers to speak to the class about what we loved to do. Immediately my hand shot into the air. No one else raised a hand except those who all of a sudden needed to go to the bathroom. I was excited to talk about the latest pirate ship I had just built. My talk was such a success that I was asked to share my story with other classes. Even then I was a natural public speaker—my second career—and anxious to share information with an audience. Now, when people ask me how long I have been on the speaking circuit, I can honestly say since I was five.

Throughout my career both as an engineer and then later

as a public speaker trainer, I have had the opportunity to write and present papers at conferences to various professionals. Early on I learned how important it was to develop my speaking skills. As a professional speaker, I now coach people from all over the world on ways to improve their speaking, presentation, and communication skills.

Regardless of your profession, you probably spent your school years training, learning, and fine-tuning your reading and writing skills. If you are like most, you spent very little time learning how to develop your public speaking skills—schools don't typically teach these skills, unless you join the debate team. However, as you will learn shortly, most communications occur on a verbal basis. Each day presents opportunities for informal and formal public speaking, from making a phone call at work to giving a new business presentation or running a meeting.

It is a common misconception that certain people are born good speakers. Yes, I agree that some people have the gift of gab—I could think of a few who have too much of a gift—and seem more natural at it. But make no mistake: Becoming a confident public speaker is achieved only by the desire to become a better speaker, followed by focused effort and a lot of practice. The good news is, your payoff will come quickly, you'll have fun along the way, and the confidence you develop will improve virtually all areas of your life.

Professional speakers, myself included, never stop practicing and honing their speaking skills. I am a better speaker today than I was five years ago and expect to continue to improve.

If you are like most people, you did *not* have a great first-time public speaking experience, and the thought of speaking in front of people scares you to death. In fact, according to the *Book of Lists,* public speaking is the greatest of all fears. More than 41 percent of people polled for the book named public speaking as their number one fear. The fear of dying is number seven on the list! I guess that means people would rather die than get up in front of a group of people to speak.

If you feel this way, you're not alone. In fact, some of today's most famous presenters have freely admitted to nervousness and stage fright when it comes to public speaking. You may be saying to yourself right now, There is no way I will be a good speaker. I can never learn to be like those professional speakers; speaking just comes easily to them. Most of us naturally worry about what other people think about us, and this is especially true when we are asked to speak to a group of people. Learning specific techniques to improve your public speaking can help eradicate your fear and help you succeed in your business and personal life.

Confidence Builder: Public Speaking Improves Every Area of Your Life

Whether you are having a casual telephone conversation, teaching a Sunday school class, having a conversation with your boss, or giving a formal presentation, you are involved in public speaking. Following are examples of how public speaking can positively influence your everyday life, your career, your relationships, your communication style, and much more. Let's get started on the path to successful public speaking.

- **Build success in your professional life.** Most presidents and CEOs of companies possess strong speaking skills. I work with many high-level executives in the business world, and when I ask them why they feel they need coaching to improve their speaking skills, they all indicate that they know their success and their companies' future business ventures rely on their ability to speak well. Their promotions to the top were related directly to their ability to communicate effectively.

- **Communicate with others more clearly.** Many mistakes or misinterpretations are a result of not properly communicating your ideas. Good public speaking skills help you articulate ideas well and make them come alive for the listener. This was one of the most critical skills I needed to develop as an engineer, because I often had to speak to audiences that didn't know the first thing about how to "shore up" a building, for example, but had the authority and the money to fund my next project. If I was ineffective in conveying why they should invest more money, I might have been out of a job.
- **Build overall confidence.** As you become better at organizing and communicating your ideas effectively, you will start to exhibit more confidence. People with this ability have a "glow" of confidence when they speak in public. (Let's not confuse this with the red glow of terror on the face of someone who is scared to death.)
- **Increase your comfort level in social situations.** How many of you have ever been invited to a party and are afraid to strike up a conversation? (Don't be shy, no one can see you.) Social situations are, in fact, the perfect opportunity to practice your public speaking skills. Here's a little bonus: It is a known fact that people who speak well are perceived as better looking. Thank God, now I know why I worked so hard at it, and it wasn't just my cute smile that made me popular with the girls.
- **Speak more confidently on the telephone.** Whether you call to request information, make a cold call at

work, communicate with a client, or just leave a phone message, others can hear your confidence level in the tone of your voice. Did you know that over 86 percent of your telephone message is communicated through the tone of your voice?

- **Run meetings or present new ideas more effectively.** I remember running my son's Cub Scout pack. Having the ability to conduct a Cub Scout meeting with six to eight screaming, energetic boys definitely challenged my public speaking skills (and required a lot of aspirin). Organizing and running a meeting with adults is more difficult, I think, because you can't bribe them with candy.
- **Become an effective member or volunteer.** At some point in your life, you may volunteer or even be affectionately coerced to lead or participate in a professional or social organization. Your success within the organization depends significantly on your ability to speak to a group and keep their attention engaged in order to achieve common goals and objectives.
- **Establish trust and respect from others with greater ease.** Your success in dealing with clients—or even your own children—depends a great deal on your speaking skills. The ability to convince people with words is key to establishing trust and respect. This can include not only what you say, but how you say it.

If these examples describe characteristics you want to possess, then congratulations—you have the desire to succeed as a public speaker.

Lessons from Mom: Practice Makes Perfect

There is no magic formula for becoming a polished public speaker. Those of you who play a musical instrument know you do not become proficient without practice. I used to roll my eyes when my mom told me to practice for an hour after school before I went outside. I later came to appreciate that time, and I continued to improve. As a semiprofessional musician (my kids may beg to differ) who has learned to play the guitar and piano, I know what steps I had to take to play these instruments well. It has been said, "To learn to play the trumpet, you have to play the trumpet." Similarly, "To learn to speak, you have to speak." You cannot become an effective communicator by just watching other great speakers. You cannot become a confident public speaker without practice, practice, and even more practice. Many of you have probably heard the two-line cliché "How do you get to Carnegie Hall?" (Answer:) "Practice, practice, practice." Public speaking demands the same level of practice. You can start right away by practicing your public speaking skills in everyday situations.

Quick Tips You Can Use in Everyday Speaking Situations

A terrific first step to developing speaking skills is to begin to focus on how you speak in everyday speaking situations. Let's take a look at four situations where you can begin to polish your speaking skills.

Running into Someone at the Store

How many of you have bumped into a friend while shopping or running an errand? Here you are—another opportunity to practice your public speaking.

- Initiate the conversation.
- Ask the person how her family is doing. What's new with her job? Does she have any vacation plans coming up?
- Tell a funny story about something that happened recently to you, your family, or your friends.
- Think about how fast you speak, how you pronounce your words, and how you organize your thoughts. This is called your natural speaking style and will come in handy later.

Parties

Parties are the perfect opportunity to practice your public speaking skills. So the next party you attend, make sure you bring your bag of tricks.

- If you find yourself standing alone in a corner of the room, don't just eat all the crab dip: Initiate a conversation with the next person who walks by.
- Introduce yourself to two new people (see "Your First Speech: 'Introducing Yourself' " later in this chapter).
- Participate in a group discussion, but do not dominate the conversation.
- Have a conversation with someone you have not seen in a while.

Leaving a Telephone Message

Doesn't it seem nowadays that you leave a message or voice mail more often than reaching someone on the phone right off the bat? Telephone tag is the new corporate sport. Consider these moments golden opportunities to practice your speaking and organization skills. The next time you need to call someone, write a few brief notes so you won't forget anything if you get the person's voice mail—and I guarantee you, you will get their voice mail.

- Slow down! Do not speak fast when you are leaving a message, especially if you have an accent. Most answering machines today allow enough time for a short message. I can't tell you the number of messages I get a day where I cannot understand what the caller is saying because he or she is speaking too fast. I often find myself replaying the message a few times. This is why notes come in handy. Also, slow down when saying your telephone number.
- Pronounce your name clearly. State your name slowly, especially if your name is not as common as Smith or Jones. Also spell your name slowly if necessary (*f* as in Friday, *t* as in ticket . . .).
- In addition to your name, give your title, your company name, and the reason you are calling. Describe to the person, in a few short sentences, the purpose of the call. If appropriate, leave the time you called (be sensitive to different time zones).
- Let them know when to return the call. Leave a date, preferred time, and telephone number.
- Always sound professional. Do not chew gum, and do not leave a long-winded message. Be aware of your tone.

I always tell people to smile when leaving a message—it automatically gives your voice an upbeat, pleasant tone.

Should the person you are calling actually answer the telephone, you can still use your notes. It will make you sound professional and organized.

Creating a Voice Mail

Even though you may not have thought about it this way, your own voice mail message is like a little presentation to the public and leaves a first impression.

- Before you record your greeting, write it down and practice saying it. Record the message, play it back, and rerecord it if necessary. Is your message too fast? Is it too slow? Is your voice clear and easy to understand? This is great practice for when you prepare your own speech.
- Make sure your answering machine greeting sounds professional and friendly. Call your own phone number and listen to your own greeting. Ask yourself if your voice is clear and your message makes sense. You would be surprised at the number of poor greetings I've heard when returning calls.
- Leave the caller clear instructions on what to do when leaving a message.
- If you run a business, as I do, your voice mail greeting is a great opportunity to plug your business. Be careful of information overload, though.

Speech Anxiety: The Doctor Is In

The problem most people face when they speak in more formal settings is keeping their focus on being conversational rather than worrying about what the audience is thinking about them. In every one of my seminars I ask participants to list the reasons they attend my program. The top vote—to quell their speaking fears. Here are seven "symptoms" of fear expressed over and over again. Any of these sound familiar?

- Sweaty palms
- Nausea
- Accelerated heart rate
- Shortness of breath
- Chest pains
- Tingling or numbness
- Anxiety or uneasiness

Most people with speech anxiety experience one or more of these symptoms. Think about a time when you experienced similar feelings. Have you ever had to make a cold call to someone? Ask someone out on a date for the first time? Explain to your boss why you think you deserve a raise? These are all situations where you may become anxious and experience some of the symptoms discussed. Everyone, even veteran speakers, experience some anxiety when speaking in front of a group of people. Let's take a look at where some of these fears originate.

First Things First—Calming Your Anxiety

During my many years as a speaker (remember, I have been doing this since I was only five), I have witnessed every kind of speech anxiety symptom. In my seminars I always present a section on techniques for dealing with these fears. Learning to overcome these feelings is critical to becoming a more confident, successful speaker.

The best way to deal with speaking anxiety is to first acknowledge that this fear is perfectly normal and you are not alone. Most studies suggest fear of public speaking is associated with a stressful childhood or early school year experience speaking in front of others. My fears were limited mostly to being beaten up by the school bully. Most people remember a specific moment in their life when they first experienced this anxiety. It may have been during one of those "show and tell" moments in school when the entire class, especially that girl or boy you had a crush on, laughed at you. We have a tendency to forget why they laughed and just remember that they did!

Most people develop speaking phobias while in middle school. This is the time when a well-meaning teacher asked you to speak in front of your class or asked you to say something in a social setting. Yet think about it. Adolescence is one of the most difficult periods in life. As a middle school student, you were going through tremendous social, emotional, and physical changes and were very sensitive to what other people thought about you, especially your fellow classmates. Unfortunately, many people carry these turbulent feelings into adulthood; thus experiences, good or bad, are etched in your mind forever.

You see, it is this fear of failure that you find yourself dealing with at one time in your life. I remember back in middle school when my best friend, Jerry, was going to talk to the entire sixth-grade class about what it is like to play drums. Jerry had made special arrangements to get into the school early so he could set up his drum set. He set up his drums quickly and was ready. When he rushed to his first-period class, he did not see his drum set. He thought someone had played a trick on him and moved it. Jerry was so nervous when he got to school, he had set up his drum set in a similar classroom on the third floor. The problem was, our classroom was on the second floor. He forgot to check which room he was really in. Needless to say, Jerry learned a good lesson. Half of a speaker's or performer's success is just showing up in the right place at the right time. Hopefully something like this has never happened to you.

Many people today who work in front of the public, such as singers, actors, and politicians, still experience, to varying degrees, these same fears. Some people call speech anxiety "stage fright." I like to think of it as "speech excitement." How you deal with it starts with what you call it. Speech excitement means positive energy.

When I survey the participants in my seminars and probe further, I find similar stories to Jerry's. You'd think I was a doctor asking about their symptoms so I can prescribe the "magic pill" to help them.

Relaxation Techniques

Let's assume that you had about ten minutes before you were scheduled to give a presentation. What can you do to help yourself relax?

Deep Breathing

One of the best exercises you can do before you speak is to practice some deep breathing techniques for about five to ten minutes. Here's how it's done:

1. Sit relaxed in your chair with your back straight and your hands dangling at your sides.
2. Let the blood flow to your fingertips and slowly inhale and exhale, taking deep breaths as you let your body relax. You can even close your eyes if you want.
3. As you breathe in, hold your breath for about three to four seconds and exhale slowly.
4. Repeat this slowly for about five minutes.

Deep breathing allows your body to take in more oxygen, which in turn acts like a natural drug to relax your muscles by forcing your body to release endorphins—chemicals in your body that act as a stimulant. This simple exercise is used by many speakers, performers, and athletes. Practice doing these exercises until you learn the proper rate and extent of deep breathing you need to relax you. Be careful not to breathe too deep, too fast, or you may find yourself getting dizzy. You do not want to hyperventilate.

Visualization

Another great technique, which you can use in conjunction with deep breathing, is "visualization." This is a simple process.

1. Close your eyes and imagine, or "visualize," yourself speaking.

2. Picture yourself speaking in a loud, clear, and assured voice, and imagine that the audience is fascinated by what you're saying.

Studies have shown that if you visualize yourself giving a successful presentation, you will be successful. Professional and Olympic skiers use visualization, too. Before they actually head down the slope, they visualize in their mind where the gates and turns are and virtually practice the course in their mind.

As a professional speaker, I use visualization all the time, visualizing and "navigating" the "course" of a speech before starting. I first visualize myself walking up to the stage as I am introduced and the audience applauding as I make my way to the podium. It is not unusual for me to arrive early to physically practice walking on stage so later my visualization process is more realistic. Some experts even suggest imagining your audience sitting nude. I don't know about you, but if I tried this with some of my previous audiences, I might get very distracted. The most important part of the visualization process is to think positive.

Positive Self-Talk

Positive self-talk is the process of associating a situation with positive results. Imagine people applauding you, not running away, as you walk on stage. Imagine your audience listening to every word you say, not snoring so loudly that even you can't hear yourself. The power of the mind is truly amazing, and those who have a positive outlook experience success, which in turn builds confidence.

Don't worry if you have trouble at first. These breathing and visualization techniques take some practice and become easier the more frequently you practice. Try all these techniques to discover which technique or combination of techniques works best for you.

Warm-up Routines

I, as well as many other professional speakers, all have "warm-up" routines. For me, it's arriving early and walking around the room where I will speak. As I said earlier, I walk to the podium or stage and even walk around the room where the audience will be sitting so I can get a feel for the room. Then I find a quiet location, out of sight from the audience, where I practice deep breathing exercises while visualizing the speaking environment. I also visualize people looking at me as my introduction is being given. As I start my speech, I like to smile at the audience and focus on my opening lines. I use this warm-up routine before each speaking engagement. It has the greatest positive effect on me—I not only relax, but I find I actually have more energy. Find a warm-up routine that works for you and begin using it regularly.

Quick Techniques for Handling Nervousness

You may not realize it, but a major portion of speech anxiety comes from nervousness. There are a variety of techniques you can start using immediately to help you deal with nervousness. Here are some that I teach clients during workshops. I have broken them into two categories: physical and mental.

Physical Techniques for Handling Nervousness

You can use these techniques to physically warm up your body.

1. Take a brisk walk before you speak. This will help loosen up your entire body and get your blood circulating. If you are speaking in a large hotel, as I often do, take a walk around the hotel and walk off some of this nervous energy. Just don't get lost, and keep your eye on the time.
2. Don't sit with your legs crossed. Stand up well in advance of being introduced and walk around so your legs will not cramp as they often do when you first stand.
3. Before you speak, while sitting in your seat, let your arms dangle at your sides and let the blood flow to the tips of your fingers. When the blood flow is directed away from your skin, fingers, and toes, you often feel a tingling sensation, and your skin may begin to look pale and feel cold. Sometimes people experience tingling or numbness because the blood flow travels to the larger muscles such as the thighs and biceps. Letting your hands dangle at your sides helps reestablish blood flow to your hands and fingertips. During this process you will start to feel better and more relaxed. You may need to stand up and walk around to get the blood flowing to your legs for the same reason.
4. Also while sitting, turn your wrists and shake your fingers to force the blood to flow to your hands and fingers.
5. Wriggle your jaw back and forth gently to help loosen up your facial muscles.
6. Scrunch your toes, but be careful not to scrunch so tightly that you get a cramp.
7. Yawn (politely, of course).
8. Use deep breathing exercises.

Mental Techniques for Handling Nervousness

Here are several mental techniques you can include as part of your warm-up routine.

1. Prepare and rehearse. This is the single most important thing you can do.
2. Think "success" using the visualization techniques.
3. Be natural but enthusiastic.
4. Visualize the audience applauding you when you are done.
5. Think conversational, and include some personal stories during your talk.
6. Focus on your message and *not* on your nervousness.

Top Ten List: Tips to Help You Overcome Speaking Anxiety

To help you get started on the right track, here's a roundup of specific tips to help you better deal with any speaking anxiety.

1. **Get ready.** Preparation is key to any speech. I like to think of it as the nine *P*'s.
   Prior Proper Preparation
   Prevents Poor Performance
   Of the Person Putting on the Presentation
2. **Think on the bright side.** Although you may think the audience will rise up and laugh at you in unison, this never happens. Use all your newly learned techniques to conquer your first and future speeches.

3. **Be aware of your speaking environment.** Arrive early and walk around the room. Stand in the location where you will give the speech, and sit in an audience seat, too.
4. **Know your listeners.** Greet audience members and chat with them. It is easier to speak to a group of friends than to a group of strangers. Arriving early provides you with the opportunity to meet people.
5. **Warm up.** You can ease some of your tension by practicing your warm-up routine.
6. **Realize people want you to succeed.** All audiences want speakers to be interesting, stimulating, informative, and entertaining. They want you to succeed, not fail.
7. **Don't apologize for being nervous.** Most of the time your nervousness will not show at all. If you don't refer to it, nobody will notice. If you mention your nervousness or apologize for any kinks you believe you have in your speech, you will only be calling attention to yourself.
8. **Concentrate on your message.** Your nervous feelings dissipate when you focus your attention away from your anxieties and concentrate on your message and your audience, not yourself.
9. **Control jitters constructively.** The same nervous energy that causes stage fright can also be an asset if you let it. Force your body to move by walking as you speak. Use your arms and hands to gesture with vitality and enthusiasm.
10. **Gain experience.** Experience builds confidence. The more you speak, the more your confidence helps dispel your anxiety. Most speakers find their anxiety decreases more after each speech.

Your Own Natural Speaking Style

Most novice speakers look at professional speakers and think to themselves, I can never speak like them. You might be tempted to copy someone else, but don't. Just be yourself, but do learn to be enthusiastic. Each speaker has his or her own way of presenting just as everyone has his or her own writing style. It's perfectly okay to study the various styles of great speakers, but also determine what you like about the way they speak and how that relates to your own style. Certain mannerisms might be very charismatic in another speaker but come across as forced or fake when you try them yourself. Trust your own judgment about what feels right.

For some reason, people feel they need to use a different voice when giving a speech. Nothing could be further from the truth. The voice that communicates the best for you in all speaking situations is your own natural conversational style, but at its most upbeat and enthusiastic. This is true whether you are speaking to a small group or a room full of hundreds of people. Okay, let's give this a try with a very short, informal kind of public speaking—introducing yourself.

Your First Speech: "Introducing Yourself"

Your first assignment is to deliver a short speech about yourself. It does not have to be very long. Since you are talking about yourself, there's no research involved. (See, that's easy.) What you do need is a game plan:

1. Think about "what" you are going to talk about—this is your content.
2. Decide in what order you will discuss items—this is your outline.

3. Begin by thinking about it as a conversation and not a speech.
4. Keep it short and sweet.

To help you get started, I have provided a short example—a brief synopsis about myself. After all, you will be my audience for the next ten days, so why not get to know a little more about me? Use this as an example and the following general outline to develop your own introduction.

1. Start off with your name.
2. Discuss where you are from.
3. Talk a little about yourself. You might include something about your work, family, interests, hobbies, or even the goals you would like to accomplish after completing this book. Tell a few funny anecdotes that help define "you," if you like—and let your own sense of humor come out.

Sample Speech: Let Me Introduce Myself

Good morning. My name is Lenny Laskowski. I'm here today to tell you about my wife and kids. I live in Connecticut and have been married for twenty-five years to my wife, Joan. I have a son, Michael, twenty-one, and a daughter, Kelly, eighteen. My wife is a learning disabilities teacher who was, I'm proud to say, the 1996 National Learning Disabilities Teacher of the Year.

My son is a senior in college, majoring in business finance. Michael has always been a good, hardworking student. He also keeps himself in great shape by working out daily. He makes me feel guilty. Michael knows more about health, taking care of your body, and how to keep fit than anyone else I know, and he is my own personal fitness trainer. But I think his biceps will always be bigger than mine. Michael plays on his college rugby team (ouch!) and truly loves his dog, Riley, a rottweiler, who we think might actually make the Olympic Frisbee team.

My daughter, Kelly, started college this year and is majoring in business and political science. Kelly has been a dancer since the age of two. Her mother and I are thinking of starting a Web site to sell all her old costumes. She is a member of the USA tap team and is a two-time world champion in tap dancing! I myself would fall flat on my face if I attempted to do such a thing. She must have gotten her talent from her maternal grandmother, who was a real pistol on the dance floor back in the twenties. We watched Kelly at her most recent performance at the America's Junior Miss competition. I will always remember what Kelly said to my wife and me after the competition: "Although I did not win any of the national college scholarships, I still came back wealthy." Kelly made friends from all over the United States and keeps in contact with them by e-mail.

As you can probably tell, I am happily married and am very proud of both my kids.

Tip of the Day

To practice developing content for informal speeches or for adding a personal touch to any speech, get out a notebook and label the top of each page with a separate category. For each one, jot down anecdotes, funny thoughts, little stories, and ideas. Many of the people I coach have told me the hardest thing for them to do is to come up with topics to speak about and icebreakers to start speeches. Here are some categories to get you started:

- Self. It's okay to be self-centered in speeches about yourself. You might include some subcategories such as travel stories, funny things that have happened to you, childhood anecdotes, things you do well, and things you love to do.
- Family. You never know, your audience may enjoy hearing how your husband took your daughter to get her license and got pulled over for speeding, causing her to miss her driving exam.
- Friends. The fact that your best friend plays the piano with her toes can really lighten up a speech.
- Neighbors. You may have a Kramer living next door whom you can use for entertainment in your speeches.

Here are a few more categories you can use:

- Work
- Hobbies and sports/interests
- Kids

Breathe a sigh of relief, you made it through Day 1. See, that wasn't so hard! In Day 2 I provide you with a road map for organizing your presentations. I give more than 120 programs a year, so trust me, I have to be organized. In addition, I offer ideas and secret tricks to spice up your speeches and give them more impact.

Day 2

Create a Great Presentation

Think of any project you want to accomplish: Getting started is probably the most difficult part of the entire process. The same applies to organizing speeches. Many people dread the process of writing and preparing a speech so much that they put it off until they find themselves two days from the actual day of the presentation—and panic sets in. Here is where some of you may have contemplated calling in sick and asking the group you will be addressing to find someone else.

However, guilt sets in and somehow you find the courage to get started, and you quickly throw together a speech or presentation. You deliver the speech the next day and manage to get through the event. Let's be honest, how many of you have actually used this "do or die" approach? Many of you, I'm sure.

You have heard the expression "Rome wasn't built in a day." Great presentations aren't built in a day, either, unless you are trying to demonstrate how *not* to prepare a presentation. In most cases it fails and you say to yourself, I will never volunteer to give a speech again.

The problem with the hasty approach is that you set yourself up for failure and then try to convince yourself that this public speaking stuff is not for you. If you had a method to quickly organize your thoughts, a way to structure your speech, and additional time to practice (practice? you say. What's that?), you would be the hit of the event. Lack of preparation, also known as waiting until the last minute, is one of the biggest contributors to the speech anxiety I discussed in Day 1. Remember from Day 1 that the number one thing you can do to help overcome your speech anxiety is to prepare. My seminar participants often ask me, "When should I start preparing for a presentation?" I always say to them, "The moment they ask you!" Here is an example:

Your boss comes up to you and says, "I would like you to prepare [there's that word again] a presentation for the new staff members on Monday and give them an overview of what our group really does—goals, objectives, the whole nine yards. I really want it to be special, and I am counting on you." Several thoughts race through your mind at this time. How can I get someone else to do this? Why couldn't he have asked someone else? Why *me?* Before you realize it, you open your mouth and the words come blurting out: "No problem, I'd love to." Somehow your mouth and brain did not talk to each other, and you find yourself agreeing! You then proceed to spend the rest of the week worrying about the speech, losing sleep over what you are going to say and how you are going to say it. Before you know it, you realize that tomorrow is the day, and you finally begin to prepare for your presentation.

This approach will not work.

The first step in creating a great presentation is to gather information. Following are examples of how I and another professional speaker gather information in preparation for presentations. Let's see what the experts have to say.

Tips from the Experts: Best Ideas for Organization

Here are some tips from Tom Antion, a member of the National Speakers Association, a respected colleague of mine, and author of *Wake 'Em Up!: How to Use Humor and Other Professional Techniques to Create Alarmingly Good Business Presentations.* Tom, like myself, travels all over the world for speaking engagements. I recommend Tom's Web site: www.antion.com.

Being able to find humor, stories, quotes, and other speech materials when you need them is very important. It is very frustrating to know you have a piece of material but can't find it. An organizational system is essential to efficient preparation.

A file and cross-reference system helps you keep track of your material. Tom uses both a computer and a hard-copy filing system. Both have advantages, so don't worry if you do not have a computer.

The Computer

Keep separate files for each topic in your presentation and also for each part and category of a speech, such as "Response to Introduction" and "Openings." Tom suggests you can do this on three-by-five-inch cards in a regular file box or cabinet if you do not have a computer.

Some information in Tom's topic files may be duplicated in other topic files. For instance, some of his signature stories, personal stories that most professional speakers include about themselves in most of their speeches, are about Tom's dog, Freeway. Tom uses Freeway stories to talk about customer service and to illustrate going the extra mile, reacting under pressure, or thinking quickly. Consequently Freeway stories show up in several of Tom's topic files.

Using a computer has many advantages. When Tom prepares for a talk, all he has to do is open the file on his speech topic and select the information he wants to use. He then copies the material to another file named for the group to whom he will be speaking, such as "Rotary Club." When traveling, Tom can take his speech reference information on a few floppy disks or a laptop computer so he can work on upcoming speeches or call up the files in case he gives another talk while on the road.

Keeping various stories in your database provides you quick access to stories that may fit the audience you are addressing. Many professional speakers complete a thorough audience analysis survey to learn as much pertinent information as possible. By having your stories properly indexed and stored on your computer, you can find everything with the click of a mouse and insert what you need in the appropriate section of your presentation. For example, if I'm talking to a group of insurance professionals, I use a story from the insurance industry. If I'm talking to a group of engineers, I use one of my own stories from my engineering days. I even clip stories from newspapers and write short summaries of the key points I want to use and store them on my computer as well. In addition, I make notes as to where I have stored the hard copy of the original newspaper article so I can easily go back and review it if I want to.

Hard Copy

Tom also uses folders in a filing cabinet to store cartoons, clippings, and so on. He organizes overhead transparencies and other audiovisual material in binders by inserting them into three-ring document protectors. You can also use three-ring pouches to hold miscellaneous items such as pencils, pens, Scotch tape, and so on.

Even though the hard-copy filing method is slower than the computer, it has two big advantages.

1. The filing cabinet has never given Tom a general message saying, "Not enough memory," or, "An error has occurred." He has never had to sit with a technician for hours while the computer is being serviced. Never once has it been difficult to find a file. It even works well during a thunderstorm or power outage.
2. Having hard files and a big box of miscellaneous material forces you to search through material to find the piece of information you need. In doing this, you are reminded of many things you forgot you had collected. Maybe it's time to review some of the old stuff.

Other Ideas for Organizing Materials

I also use a filing system where I collect quotes and humorous stories, record personal anecdotes, and keep clippings of interesting magazine articles on a variety of topics. I arrange these files according to topics. Since I speak to organizations for various industries, I collect material about everything from aerospace to zoology, including information such as

- what challenges each industry is facing;
- significant changes in that industry;
- the latest rumors about that industry can be included in a presentation.

If I'm scheduled to speak to a corporation, I usually ask them to send me

- company newsletters, publications, or annual reports, so I can learn more about that company's issues and outlook, as well as the corporate culture, before I speak to them. I do this thorough search several weeks or months before the actual presentation.

Before I leave for my presentation, whether it's the day of the presentation or the evening before, I

- read national newspapers and skim for up-to-the-minute news I can use during my presentation.

When I arrive at my destination I

- buy a local newspaper and look up any local news I can also include in my presentation. Incorporating current events impresses your audience.

When you are gathering materials, the idea is to have more material than you will be able to cover in your allotted time. To be an authority in front of your audience, you should know at least ten times as much about your topic as the audience does. I also recommend collecting

- personal anecdotes that show your creative or humorous side. Also think about the times you made mistakes and how you can relate these mistakes to your topic. Be prepared to share your life experiences. Can you remember the time you made a fool of yourself? Can you laugh at that now? Turn childhood experiences into stories you can share with your audience.

Quick Tips to Start Organizing Information About Yourself

A good way to start organizing stories about yourself is with your family. Include stories about your parents, your children, your pets, your neighbors. Think back to your childhood and school days. Jot down notes about experiences that have happened to you in your life, good, bad, and unusual; funny, dramatic, expected, and unexpected.

The idea is to gather as much material as you can and start to record and organize it into categories. The same approach works well when preparing your actual speech. The key is to collect as much data as possible, whether you use it or not.

For example, I keep a little notepad in my car or pocket so I can write down ideas that I might be able to use later. Take a small notepad and pencil when you are exercising. Some of the greatest ideas have come to me while walking on the treadmill or around my neighborhood. Having a spot to write down these ideas the minute you think of them is a plus. If you think you will remember them when you get home, think again.

Recording these ideas a few weeks ahead helps you better prepare for the speech. Try to write down how these ideas relate to the audience and your presentation. This proven method alleviates the pressure from having to start from scratch.

Speech Preparation as a Process

Genuine speech preparation means looking within yourself. You need to gather facts and arrange these facts in conjunction with your thoughts. It is not enough simply to collect ideas. You must also nurture and reflect on them and decide how to present the ideas in a unique, organized manner. I will go into more detail on the structure of your speech later in the chapter. Following are some tips to get you started preparing for your next speech or presentation. Whether you are talking to a small group or addressing a large auditorium of people, these tips will put you on the path to successful speech giving.

- A speech needs time to grow—prepare for weeks.
- Sleep on your topic, dream about it, and let your ideas sink into your subconscious.
- Ask yourself questions.
- Write down your thoughts.
- Keep adding new ideas.

Once you have determined the purpose (to expand your audience's knowledge of eighteenth-century law) for delivering this speech, state the purpose in a sentence (write it down) and focus your speech around it. Ask yourself, How does this purpose relate to the audience? Write down your answers. Let your purpose drive your speech. A good speech title doesn't hurt, either. Aim not only to inform your listeners, but also to persuade them. Here are a few Web sites that feature great speech titles from history:

- www.freedomvision.com/famousspeeches/home.html
- http://douglass.speech.nwu.edu/
- http://www.tamu.edu/scom/pres/archive.html

Structuring Your Speech

As you prepare each speech, choose a simple structure:

- **Sequential.** Will the material follow chronological order or how the events happened?

- **Categorical.** Will the speech be structured according to the categories? If so, will you talk about the most important category first or last?
- **Problem and solution.** Will your speech be designed to state a dilemma and then offer a device to address the problem?
- **Contrast and comparison.** Will your speech discuss similarities and differences between/among your main points?

Outline

Regardless of its length, your speech should contain the following main sections:

1. The introduction
2. The body
3. The conclusion

Let's take a look at each of these three sections in detail.

- **The Introduction.** The introduction actually consists of three parts: the introductory grabber, the purpose, and the agenda. The introductory grabber is an opening—a pertinent quote or some shocking information or statistics. You can even start with something humorous. The purpose of the speech should focus on the benefits to the listeners. Most listeners want to know "What's in it for me?" The purpose answers that question. The agenda highlights the points that you will cover in your speech.
- **The Body.** This is the meat of your speech or presentation, where you present and discuss the main ideas. The number of points you choose to discuss

depends on the length of your speech. Here are some general guidelines on the number of main points you should discuss given a certain length of time.

Time Limit	*Main Points to Cover*
20 minutes	4
30 minutes	4–6
60 minutes	6–8

If you remember in my sample speech in Day 1, I briefly discussed my wife, Joan; my son, Michael; and my daughter, Kelly. The level of detail was brief but to the point. I could easily have expanded on any of that information to make a longer speech. The structure would remain the same, but the level of detail would increase.

- **The Conclusion.** Your conclusion serves as a brief review and should leave the listeners thinking about what you said. It is usually divided into three parts:
  1. **The review.** This section reiterates the purpose of the speech and highlights the answers to the audience's question "What's in it for me?"
  2. **The call to action.** During this segment, tell the audience what to do with the information you've presented.
  3. **The closing grabber.** This consists of your closing remarks and should leave listeners with at least one memorable thought.

Picking Apart a Speech

Let's take my short sample speech example provided in Day 1 and see how to identify the main message, objectives, purpose, central ideas, conclusion, and so on.

Here's the introduction of my speech. See if you can find the purpose and agenda of this speech.

Introduction

"Good morning. My name is Lenny Laskowski. I'm here today to tell you about my wife and kids. I live in Connecticut and have been married for twenty-five years to my wife, Joan. I have a son, Michael, twenty-one, and a daughter, Kelly, eighteen."

I included a statement that provided the main purpose of my speech at the beginning of the introduction: "I'm here today to tell you about my wife and kids."

I then gave a transitional statement that leads into specific details about my family. The transitional statement is, "I live in Connecticut and have been married for twenty-five years to my wife, Joan. I have a son, Michael, twenty-one, and a daughter, Kelly, eighteen."

I then proceed to give a brief description or statement about my wife, my son, and my daughter—that's the body.

Body

Now examine the crux of my speech. You will see that the major portion of the speech focuses on my family.

"My wife is a learning disabilities teacher who was, I'm proud to say, the 1996 National Learning Disabilities Teacher of the Year.

"My son is a senior in college, majoring in business finance. Michael has always been a good, hardworking student. He also keeps himself in shape by working out daily. . . .

"My daughter, Kelly, started college this year and is majoring in business and political science. Kelly has been a dancer since the age of two. Her mother and I are thinking of starting a Web site to sell all her old costumes. She is a member of the USA tap team and is a two-time world champion in tap dancing! . . ."

Conclusion

I end the speech with a brief statement about my family.

"As you can probably tell, I am happily married and am very proud of both my kids."

Remember, it is not always necessary to have long closings, especially with very short speeches. With all speeches you want to conclude by highlighting the main points, discussing each briefly and giving a synopsis of what the audience has learned.

Five-Step Approach to Developing Speech Content

For many people, developing speech content is a very difficult task. What will I talk about? How will I make interesting points? In my seminars I talk about the fact that getting started is the hardest aspect of preparing a speech and the main reason people procrastinate. Most people spend too much time worrying about how they are going to begin their speech. My advice is to plan your introduction last; focus on the body of the speech first.

Following are the steps I recommend for developing speech content. As an example, here is how I used these steps to help a client develop an educational speech entitled "Preparing Students for the 21st Century." The objective of the speech was to identify the top ten skills students need to succeed in the twenty-first century.

1. **Gather all the information possible on the subject.** Also, look for little details you think may be useful. Try the Internet for resource material by typing key words related to your topic into several search engines. Take notes on your different resources, and group information into specific folders. For this particular speech I interviewed educators over the phone and gathered their thoughts and ideas on the skills students need to thrive in the new millennium. Since my wife, Joan, is a learning disabilities teacher with over twenty-five years of experience, I also asked for her opinions and input. Then we both sat down and listed the skills we wanted our own kids to achieve.

   Here are some of the resources I found to expand my knowledge on the subject:

   - An article by Robert Kizlik I found on-line titled "Connective Transactions—Technology and Thinking for the 21st Century," www.adprima.com/connecti.htm. This article focuses primarily on the importance of mastering technology. It includes an example illustrating that without sophisticated technology, many modern surgical procedures would be impossible.
   - After speaking with a contact I had at the National Academy of Sciences, I was given this article titled "Preparing for the 21st Century—Science and Technology Policy in a New Era." The article discusses the goals of the National Academy of Sciences and zeroes in on the importance of mastering basic research skills and how people need a solid education in science, mathematics, and technology to prepare for today's workforce.

- An informative article I found on-line titled "Skills Needed for the 21st Century" from the American Chamber of Commerce Executives, www.acce.org. The article discusses the specific knowledge, skills, and behaviors students need to succeed in the new millennium.

2. **Analyze the information you have grouped or categorized to determine what information you want to use.** How much material you use depends on the length of your speech. If you are asked to speak for five minutes, the amount of material you will use is considerably less than if you are asked to speak for thirty minutes.
3. **Organize the information you want to present in coherent sequence.** At this point don't concern yourself with the length of your presentation. Rather, make sure that your speech follows a logical order. I sat with my client and we analyzed all the resource material to form a list of ten objectives for students.
4. **Prioritize the most important points in your speech.** Try to determine how long it will take you to talk about each point based on the information you have gathered. My client and I looked at the list we had developed in step three, and this helped us create a time frame and chronological sequence for his presentation. We then developed slide copy—one slide for each item in the list, with two or three points under each.
5. **Fine-tune the organization of your presentation content with the following approach:**
   - Tell your audience what your presentation will cover.
   - Highlight or "preview" a few main points to capture their interest.

- Begin your presentation.
- Conclude with summary points that you want your audience to remember.

Here is the list of ten objectives—the body of the speech—that my client presented, along with his main talking points.

1. **Oral and written communication skills.** Communication skills cover far more than spelling and grammar. Students need to develop the ability to communicate effectively with the entire world. In business communications that may include everything from internal memos to business letters to formal speeches and e-mail. As cyberspace grows and cable systems expand, digital communication provides instant global access. The Internet has truly made this a smaller world, a world in which we must become more diverse in the way we think, reason, and exchange information.
2. **Critical thinking, reasoning, and problem-solving skills.** "Problem-solving skills" almost seems an ambiguous term. After all, no two problems are identical or require the same solution. Problem solving, then, requires a range of abilities that work in conjunction with one another, such as listening, communicating, critical analysis, research, and creativity.

   We hear a lot these days about the need for critical thinking skills in the workplace, but we don't hear a lot about how students can acquire these skills. I believe that courses in the humanities, such as literature, philosophy, composition, and history, which require written and verbal analysis, will provide ideal circumstances for our students to develop their analytical abilities.

While critical thinking is important, so is creative thinking, or what many refer to as "thinking outside the box." Being able to identify, analyze, and construct a solution to a problem is a skill we all need to succeed. Individuals with imagination and ambition will discover that the greatest source of wealth will be the ideas in their head.

3. **Ethical skills.** Many of us have difficulty defining the term *ethics,* yet most education experts agree that we need to nurture a firmer commitment to ethics in students. To survive and prosper in the twenty-first century, students also need self-discipline, which entails an ethical code and the ability to set and assess progress toward their own goals. By introducing students to ethics through specific applications and in relation to specific fields, we can render a more relevant component of civil life that often remains unexamined and unexplored.
4. **Use of computers and other technical skills.** The use of computers and technology has become an important—indeed, practical—part of today's workforce. Technology will most likely play a vital role in redesigning education systems in the twenty-first century. Commerce on the Internet is driven by computing and telecommunications technology. Experts predict that in 2007 the basic home computer will have 4,000 megabytes of RAM and 300,000 megabytes of storage. The Internet is bringing into every home an astonishing array of learning and commercial opportunities.

5. **Teamwork skills.** Job success relies on interpersonal, human relations skills and the ability to work as part of a team. Working together is an art that requires practice and expertise. Humanities courses can offer a range of opportunities for students to develop teamwork skills. The workforce of tomorrow will be more diverse than today. Our ability to develop interpersonal skills will continue to play a vital role, even with the surge in home-based businesses and increased emphasis on technology. Interpersonal skills will divide the workers from the achievers.
6. **Adaptability and flexibility skills.** In a fast-changing world students need a catalog of skills that are broad and deep enough to enable them to adapt to changing circumstances and to develop attitudes that encourage flexibility. Those students who learn to adapt as the business world changes will continue to succeed. Managing yourself in a world of uncertainty, opportunity, and rapid change will be the greatest challenge in the next ten years.
7. **Conflict resolution and negotiation skills.** It is essential that all elementary and high school curricula incorporate conflict resolution skills. The curriculum should provide skill-building activities that will give students practice in preventing, defusing, and avoiding conflicts. Students need to learn how to control anger, listen, and work toward a solution with their peers. These skills play a vital role in succeeding in many areas of life, including the workforce.
8. **Conduct research, interpret and apply data.** Schools need to offer ready access to the world of information through print, electronic, and face-to-face channels. These will provide students with opportunities to test

their theories based on what they discover. The United States of America must continue to remain among the world's leaders in every major area of research. A special emphasis must be placed on the development of human resources such as preparing scientists and engineers for a broad range of careers.

9. **Multiple languages skills.** Communicating effectively in more than one language is important as the marketplace becomes more international. The Internet has already made the world smaller. Speaking another language will be crucial for economic growth and world peace, as well as knowing, appreciating, and working with our global neighbors.
10. **Reading and comprehension skills.** Along with reading are listening, speaking, writing, and thinking skills. Reading is basic to all other areas of the curriculum. Reading is the foundation upon which all other skills are built. Without the right foundation students will have a more difficult time reaching their potential.

Lessons from Mom: Clean Up That Clutter

Writing a short, concise speech that is to the point is not always easy. Many times it's necessary to write the speech and then go back and revise the speech to eliminate extra, unnecessary information.

Mark Twain, the famous author and speaker, was quoted as saying, "If you want me to give you a two-hour presentation, I am ready today. If you want only a five-minute speech, it will take me two weeks to prepare." This is so true. A short speech that gets your message across effectively often will take more work than a longer speech, since the words you use need to be chosen carefully. I can remember that when I wanted to ask my parents for something, I would ramble on and on, and my mother would say, "Get to the point." You may find that when you speak you tend to use a lot of extra words to say what you really mean. You need to learn how to eliminate your own verbal clutter and speak clearly.

Hints for Eliminating Visual or Verbal Clutter

These tips will help you become more aware of your speaking manner:

- Before you begin to speak, think about the words you want to use.
- Think about what you want to say before you open your mouth.
- When you find yourself saying ahs and ums (verbal clutter), stop yourself and repeat the sentence, this time replacing the ahs and ums with silence.
- Use the pause as an effective technique. Work hard at replacing this verbal clutter with a simple pause, and during these short pauses allow your mind to catch up and think about what you want to say next.

Practice some of these quick tricks in everyday speaking situations such as making a phone call or running into someone at a bank or store, but this time focus on replacing your verbal clutter with silence.

Confidence Builder: Secrets to Give Your Public Speaking More Impact

The secret to a great presentation is to tell a story. Think back to when you were a kid and your mother or father read you a bedtime story. Kids love stories, and so do adults. People love speakers who tell stories that apply to their message. These personal stories help drive your message home. To tell your "story" effectively, follow these steps:

- **Begin at the end of your speech.** As Stephen Covey says in his book *The 7 Habits of Highly Effective People,* "Begin with the end in mind." Think about that main message you want people to understand. Then gather the facts and information you believe are pertinent to your message. Recall personal stories when you were a kid, a teenager, or a young adult that you might use.
- **Use examples your audience can relate to.** For example, if you are talking about the latest advance in cardiac medicine, you may want to share a brief story of a patient who benefited from the technology or therapy.
- **Practice telling your anecdotes as if you were telling the story for the first time.** As you practice, experiment with different phrases and ways of illustrating your story or example. The best approach is to put yourself in the story and pretend you are the main character of the story. Pretend you are acting in a play, and do some role or character playing. Try to take on the personalities and characters in your story. Use actual names or fictitious names to help define the characters in your story.
- **Practice each of your stories separately and record them.** Get a good idea of how long each story takes. This can vary depending on the level of detail you use.

> First develop a long version and then a short version of your story. This will come in handy if you need to adjust your speech time. Figure out what kinds of gestures might be used to add some dynamics to your story, such as a change in your voice, how you will move, or whether sitting or standing would be more effective. I will go into storytelling in greater detail in Day 5, where I will discuss body language and voice.

Remember, *tell them what you are going to tell them.* You can't do this until you have figured out what you will be talking about. *Tell them*—this is where the meat of your speech is—your stories, and *tell them what you told them*—this is where you do a quick review at the end, telling them what your stories were supposed to tell them, just in case they did not automatically figure it out for themselves.

Positive Performance: Effectively Structuring Your Speech Within the Allotted Time

One of the very last things you do when preparing and organizing your speech is to make adjustments in your timing. To do this effectively, make an audiotape or videotape of your speech and note how long each section of your speech took you to present. To record your speech at this point, set up your video camera or turn on your cassette recorder when you are ready and give your entire speech as if you were doing it for a live audience. It is amazing how many people *never* even record their presentations and use them as part of their practice. Many people never even practice their speech at all, and they wonder why they have too much speech left over at the end of their time allotment.

You will use this same taping technique throughout this

book. For the purpose of this chapter, you need only record the start and end times for each section of your speech. Write down the times and keep your notes handy.

I recommend the following general time guidelines for each section:

- The introduction (10 to 15 percent)
- The body (70 to 80 percent)
- The conclusion (10 to 15 percent)

Let's look at an actual example:

Say you are asked to give a speech with a 10-minute time frame. Using the higher percentages just listed, you should allow 15 percent of 10 minutes, or 1½ minutes, for your introduction and 1½ minutes for your conclusion. This leaves only 7 minutes for the actual body of your presentation. If you want a question and answer (Q&A) period at the end of your presentation, you need to allocate additional time for it. Let's say you allow for a 2-minute Q&A session at the end of your presentation. You now have 8 minutes for your presentation. This brings you to your first reality check; with 1½ minutes each for your introduction and conclusion, you now in fact have only 5 minutes for your content (body of speech)—not the 10 minutes you originally assumed.

Over my years as a professional speech coach, I have witnessed how most presenters do not use this simple math exercise when preparing their presentations. It is not a surprise to me when they actually run out of time or, worse, run well beyond their allotted time. They may have estimated ten minutes' worth of material, but they did not allow the necessary time for their introduction, conclusion, or Q&A session.

Now here is step two. Seeing that you have only five minutes for the actual body of your talk, let's also assume you will be using three stories you developed. The first question to ask yourself is, "Can I tell the three stories in the five minutes?" If not, consider using only two stories or maybe just one. Look at your videotape. Let's say it shows that story one took three minutes, story two took four minutes, and story three took six minutes. That is a total of thirteen minutes! But you have allotted only five minutes. You have a few decisions to make at this point:

- If you really want to use all three stories, can you shorten them so their combined total is less than five minutes? Keep in mind you will also need to provide a summary of the main message for each story. Even if that summary is only twenty to thirty seconds, you will need at least one minute for summaries, leaving you really only four minutes.
- In this case, I suggest using only two stories, since most stories cannot be told effectively in less than two minutes. You now need to decide on which two stories to tell. I recommend you always include your personal story and present it last. You now have four minutes to use between the two stories.
- I suggest you keep the first story very short (only about one to two minutes) and allow yourself the two to three minutes for your personal story.

Cutting Story Length

Assume that you will use story one and story three, your personal story. You see that initially it took three minutes for story one and five minutes to tell your personal story. You now need to cut each of these stories in half. Here is how you do this.

Go back and review the tape of each story and write down the main ideas discussed and the sequence of the ideas used in your original version. Notice the level of detail you used for each idea or section of your story. Decide if you can eliminate any sections or details altogether or determine how you can retell that section of the story in a more concise manner. If you haven't noticed, this is a lot of work! I didn't say it would be easy. Rerecord the story and see how your time has improved. Repeat this process for each story, paying attention to what parts of your stories can be told with less detail. Make mental or written notes during this process because you can use this information later when you are asked to give the same speech but are given more time.

The key is not to change the structure of your speech, but to reduce the level of detail. This is why it takes longer to prepare a shorter presentation than a longer one, because you need to constantly refine and rework your story, using fewer words and details but still keeping it intact. Rerecord your entire speech and address the timing again, making additional adjustments as needed. Remember, you will have to work harder at sounding natural if you are modifying personal stories that you are comfortable relaying in detail with no time constraints.

Tip of the Day

With every new speech I develop, I always prepare a ninety-minute version, a sixty-minute version, a thirty-minute version, and even a five-minute version. There are a couple of reasons why I prepare four different versions of my speeches. Often I'm asked to deliver a speech on the same topic to more than one organization or company. For instance, one client may ask me to speak for sixty minutes, and another client may want me to speak for only forty-five minutes. By having different versions of the same speech, I can easily adjust my presentation to fit the time allotment. Another reason is that many times the planned time slot for you to speak and the actual time slot available are different, such as when the presenter before you speaks too long.

I was faced with a similar predicament not too long ago when I was hired as the opening keynote speaker for a meeting being held in a hotel. My original presentation was scheduled for sixty minutes. Just before I was introduced, the fire alarm sounded and we all had to exit the building. Fortunately it turned out to be a false alarm. However, by the time we were allowed to reenter the meeting room, a half hour had passed. I was scheduled to end my speech at ten A.M.; it was now nine-thirty. I asked the meeting coordinator how she wanted me to proceed.

Since I was paid to give a sixty-minute keynote, I told her I could move forward with that presentation or give a shortened version. She asked me if I could deliver the shortened version and still motivate the audience. I gave a twenty-five minute version, which was not only a success, but helped put the seminar back on schedule. As a result, I was hired on the spot to come back the following year to give both the opening and closing keynote addresses because the meeting organizers knew I would exceed their expectations.

In Day 3 I will provide you with tools to help you relate to and analyze your audience so you can create a speech tailored to their needs and interests.

Day 3

Relating to Your Audience

You now know the importance of properly preparing your material far enough in advance so you have sufficient time to rehearse and fine-tune your speech. Preparation alone, however, does not guarantee that your speech or presentation will be well received. You must also analyze and relate to your audience.

Audience Analysis—It's Your Key to Success

Many speakers overlook the need to include any kind of audience analysis as part of their speech preparation. Proper audience analysis makes it possible for you to give the most effective, meaningful, and memorable speech to your audience. Most professional speakers send their clients, the person or company/organization representative who hired the speaker, a multipage questionnaire in order to gather information about the client and the speaking engagement. Having this information allows you to customize your presentation or speech for maximum impact. Using the word

AUDIENCE as an acronym, I have provided two sets of audience analysis questions, as well as ideas and tips on how you can use the results to customize your speeches. Let's assume that you have been asked by IDEA (the International Dance and Exercise Alliance) to speak at an upcoming sports and fitness conference in New York. What do you need to do to get started? There are two phases of audience analysis: the preprogram survey and the customized program survey. Both address the following areas that spell out the acronym *AUDIENCE.*

- ***A*nalysis.** Who is your audience? How many will be attending your presentation?
- ***U*nderstanding.** What is their knowledge about the subject on which you plan to speak?
- ***D*emographics.** Where are they from? What is their age, sex, and educational background?
- ***I*nterest.** Why will they be attending the conference/convention/event? Who asked them to attend, or will they be participating of their own accord?
- ***E*nvironment.** Where will you stand? Will everyone be able to see and hear you?
- ***N*eeds.** What are their needs with respect to the speech topic?
- ***C*ustomized.** What do you need to address in your speech (examples, issues, and so on) to meet the audience's needs?
- ***E*xpectations.** What do you think they expect to learn or hear from you?

Preliminary Analysis: What You Need to Know

To help you develop a better idea of the type of information you need for audience analysis, here's a detailed list of information you need to gather about your audience. Both surveys can be done by mail, by fax, or over the telephone.

Preprogram Survey

The preprogram survey provides general information about your audience. The survey gives you a start on your audience analysis and may even help you pick your topic or angle for your speech. The survey is designed to help you prepare the best presentation possible for your audience. Before doing my survey, I usually call the client or client's representative to get to know him or her better and get a feel for what the client's needs are. Begin working on your preprogram when you are asked to give a presentation; don't wait until the last minute. Here is the preprogram survey:

1. What is the audience's knowledge and level of vocabulary on the topic? Does the audience have expert knowledge, some knowledge, or very little knowledge?
2. How large is the audience? What does the room look like where I will be speaking? What are the options for using visual aids?
3. Is this event focused around a special project or event?
4. Will there be other speakers before or after me on the program?
5. Will there be drinking or eating before my presentation?

6. Have other speakers addressed this audience on a similar topic?
7. If so, what has the audience responded to most positively?
8. What has the audience responded to least positively?
9. What kind of data, information, and support will persuade your audience?
10. What is your group's major needs, problems, and concerns?
11. How much time will I have to speak?
12. What is their relationship to me as a speaker?
13. What is their level of education?
14. What is the ratio of men to women?
15. What are their ages or range of ages?
16. What is their ethnic background?
17. What is their religion?
18. What is their occupation or profession?

The responses from your survey give you a better idea what to expect from your audience and what challenges you have planning your presentation. I rely on the results of the preprogram survey to give me the opportunity to add or modify materials to my program.

Customized Program Survey

The customized survey is more in-depth, asking specific questions about the members of the organization and letting you know any information to avoid speaking about. Begin your customized program survey when you have chosen your topic and completed the nitty-gritty of your outline. At this point, it's appropriate to recontact your liaison for the presentation about this survey. Some of the customized program survey questions are similar to the preprogram survey; that's intentional.

1. What is the theme of the meeting?
2. What are the top challenges or problems faced by members of the group?
3. What, approximately, are the characteristics of your average member?

   Age: ______ Annual Income: ______

   Educational Background: ______

   Sex: ______ Occupation: ______
4. Will there be any other special guests?
5. How many people will be in the audience?
6. Why is this group attending this meeting?
7. How will they be notified?
8. What is the audience's overall opinion regarding this subject? (favorable, hostile, etc.)
9. What three facts should I know about the group before addressing them?
10. What speakers have you used in the past, and what did they discuss?
11. What speakers/programs have been most enthusiastically received?
12. Please list the names and positions of three people in your organization who are well known and well liked within the group who will be present during my speech.
13. Whom can I call on or joke with if the need arises?

14. What are the three most significant events that have occurred in your industry, or within your group, during the past year?
15. Please share any local "color" you can think of that relates to the location where my speech will be held.
16. Specifically, what are you trying to accomplish at this meeting?
17. What are your specific objectives for my part of the meeting?
18. Are there any issues/topics in particular that you think I should discuss during the program?
19. Are there any issues/topics in particular that you think I should avoid during the program?
20. Do you have any suggestions to help me make this presentation the best your audience has ever heard?

Again, the responses help you tailor your presentation to the audience. It is up to you to develop your own list of specific questions to use for preparing your program. Take the lists I have just provided and adapt them to your own needs. Remember, the more you know about your audience the better.

Here is an example of how I used responses from both surveys to help me prepare a better presentation. The MacDermid Corporation, a firm based in Waterbury, Connecticut, was conducting a four-day training program for their international sales force and engineers, and I was asked to be the closing keynote speaker. My job as keynote speaker was to motivate the sales force and company engineers to apply the skills they learned over the course of the training.

The training program was being held at Mt. Snow, a ski resort in New England. I called Mt. Snow and found out the name of their most challenging black diamond slope, Jaws of

Death. I also made plans to arrive the evening before to get to know the names of as many participants as possible. During my keynote, I compared the challenges of preparing a presentation to the challenges of skiing down a mountain—how sometimes you fall, but you force yourself to get back up and try again. I incorporated into my presentation the name of their CEO, who was sitting in the front row and had a great sense of humor. I used a comical ending that involved the use of a ski hat, gloves, and goggles. This illustrated that you can take risks and entertain at the same time if you use a story to drive your message home.

By tying in to my speech the message and location of their meeting, relating the challenges of the ski slope, and personalizing my presentation with humor and audience names, I was able to customize my speech and more forcefully drive my message home. It was a success.

Remember, it is crucial to use both surveys when preparing for any presentation. Here's why:

- The preprogram survey gives a general idea of the needs of the group. For example, let's say you were giving a presentation on women in the workforce. From your survey you learned that a majority of the women were working mothers.
- The customized survey gives you the necessary details about the people who will be attending your speech so you can tailor the talk to their needs. For example, you could tailor your speech to discuss how women juggle working and raising a family.

Positive Performance: The Psychology of Audiences

When an audience is invited to hear a speaker, they seldom walk into that presentation hoping the speaker is boring or fails miserably. When was the last time you went to a seminar and said to yourself, I hope I get nothing out of this seminar and I won't mind if I wasted my money? What you are more likely to say is, I hope this seminar provides some valuable information, insight, specific tools, or techniques I can start using today to help me with my job.

An audience wants to feel that your speech, seminar, or presentation has direct relevance to them. People may be looking for answers to help them with problems they have at home or at work. An audience wants to feel that you care about and understand them.

This is where your audience analysis comes in handy. The more in-depth your audience analysis questions, the more prepared you are to understand the psychology of your audience, their needs, and their desires. Knowing this specific information prepares you with the information you need to address these needs during your presentation and have the audience say on your evaluation sheet, "This presenter really understood my problems and was right on the money!" The key to being a successful public speaker is to properly know your audience *before* you speak to them.

Tips from the Experts: The Seven Subconscious Desires of Your Audience

Tony Jeary, author of *Inspire Any Audience,* provides what he calls the "Seven Subconscious Desires of Your Audience" relevant to giving a speech everyone in your audience wants to hear. They are the following:

1. To belong
2. To be respected
3. To be liked
4. To be safe
5. To succeed
6. To be inspired
7. To be romanced

This means from your audience's viewpoint, your speech or presentation has to answer a simple question: "What's in it for me?"

Confidence Builder: "Report Talk vs. Rapport Talk."

Report talk is delivering your speech in a monotone, flat voice. Often you sound as if you are just reading your speech without any effort to engage your audience. Rapport talk, on the other hand, is delivering your speech in a conversational, lively style. Building rapport with your audience is extremely critical for gaining acceptance. Before I provide you with tips for building a rapport with your audience, I want you first and foremost to realize that you must respect your audience. Treat your audience the way they would expect to be treated by their family, friends, and co-workers by being courteous and attentive to their questions and requests.

- **Greet your audience.** One of the most effective strategies I use at my seminars is to greet people as they enter the room. This demonstrates that you are accessible and approachable. I make sure I arrive early enough so everything is set up properly. By doing this, I'm able to greet people and help establish an immediate connection.

- **Begin on time.** If you are scheduled to start at nine A.M. and 90 percent of the seminar attendees are present, then start on time. Many speakers believe they should wait a few minutes to allow *everyone* to get there, but don't. You show respect to those people who went the extra mile to arrive early and on time. Why should they have to wait?
- **Recognize people by name.** If possible, I try to remember the audience names by encouraging them to wear their name tag. This lets you call on people by their names and makes the environment more personal.
- **Establish eye contact.** They say the eyes are the mirror to the soul, and having good eye contact with your audience demonstrates your true interest in them. This is especially true if you are engaged in a one-on-one conversation with an audience member. Make eye contact with as many people in your audience as possible. Be careful not to talk to the same few people in the front row.
- **Pay attention.** When people ask you a question or offer comments during the seminar, show them respect by paying close attention to what they have to say. Repeat the question for the entire audience. For example, you could say, "Mary from . . . just asked me a question about . . ." This shows respect to Mary, and you use her name.

- **Schedule breaks.** Giving the audience a break allows them to attend to personal business such as calling in to their office, and it gives them a rest, but it also allows you time to mingle with people in the audience and get to know them better. Through impromptu conversations, you can gauge the audience's reactions to the program up to that point. Tell people what time to be back from breaks.
- **Reward people for suggestions.** I have delivered many seminars where someone in the audience really participates and makes a valuable or thought-provoking suggestion that in some way has enriched the seminar. As an incentive to encourage people to participate, I give volunteers a small gift that is related to speaking or presentation skills and something they can use in their own presentations, such as one of my videotapes or audiotapes or colored markers.
- **Make yourself available.** I make it a policy to be accessible by phone, fax, and e-mail to people who attend my seminars. This gives them the opportunity to ask more questions and shows that I really care about their learning.

Please, God, Don't Let Me Be Boring

So far you've learned about audience analysis surveys, how to greet the audience, and how to establish a relationship with your audience before your program begins. Now that you have them seated before you, you don't want to put them to sleep. Following are tips and secrets to help keep your audience awake and alert.

1. **Use transitions effectively.** Transitions are an effective part of a smooth-flowing presentation, yet many speakers forget to plan their transitions. The primary purpose of a transition is to lead your listener from one idea to another. Following are a few examples that work well.
   - **Bridge words or phrases.** These include "furthermore, meanwhile, however, in addition, finally, and so on." However, try not to overuse these phrases.
   - **Point by point.** "I've made three points to remember. The first one is . . . , the second one is . . . , and the last one is . . ."
   - **Pause.** Even a simple pause, when used effectively, can act as a transition. This allows the audience to think about what was said and gives them time to register that message before addressing something new.
2. **Keep the audience involved with each other.** Allow each participant the opportunity to be involved with your presentation by giving all participants things to do during the presentation, such as greeting the person next to them or asking another audience member a question. Here are a couple of other examples to keep your audience involved:
   - **Ask a question.** "How many of you . . . ?"
   - **Flashback.** "Do you remember what I said about . . . ?"
3. **Move around.** Don't stand in one spot when you speak. Move around and force the audience to follow you with their eyes. This keeps their attention focused on you.
4. **Smile.** This universal gesture is understood by everyone in the world. It works like a charm.

5. **Establish good eye contact.** Make an effort to establish eye contact with each member in your audience; just as it helps you build rapport, it also keeps your audience engaged. The intent is not to stare at them when you are speaking, but to look at them long enough to make a connection, usually about three to five seconds per person.
6. **Involve your audience mentally.** Ask thought-provoking questions. Forcing them to think about questions you ask engages their thought process and allows them to do more than just listen.
7. **Involve your audience physically.** Give your audience creative physical exercises to do, such as stretching their arms over their heads or dangling their arms at their sides. This gets their blood flowing and their bodies involved with your presentation.
8. **Give your audience clear directions.** Provide your audience with clear instructions on what you want them to do. If they are confused, some will tune you out or get bored. Confusion is a close cousin to boredom—and both are deadly to your presentation.
9. **Conduct a verbal survey.** Make sure the entire room is benefiting from your presentation by asking them periodically during the program if they have any questions or comments. Don't just wait until the end—it might be too late! Also take this opportunity to survey the audience to ask them about their comfort (too warm, too cold, need a break for a cold drink, and so on).
10. **Interact with your audience.** Audiences love it when a seminar leader or speaker takes the time to have a conversation with them. This also gives you the

opportunity to learn more about your audience, such as their professional responsibilities, personal life, or hobbies.

Tips from the Experts: Types of Audiences

Professional speaker David Freeborn tailors his speeches in relation to these four types of audiences:

- *The Prisoner.* This is the person who does not particularly want to be at the seminar. In fact, he would rather be anywhere than indoors listening to another talk. Unfortunately, someone else—his boss—made that decision by sending him to the seminar. Freeborn says, "We welcome all prisoners because that only means they are not responsible for being here today . . . but are responsible for what they take out of here! May I see a show of hands as to how many prisoners we have here today?"
- *The Vacationer.* This is the person who volunteers to go to any seminar, figuring it's better to be in a meeting than at work, home, or somewhere else. In other words, vacationers are happy to be here, but for the wrong reasons. Freeborn says, "And we're happy to have our vacationers on board today because they like to have fun, and we'll count on them to help us have a good time. How many vacationers do we have with us today?"
- *The Graduate.* This is the person who thinks she doesn't need to be there because she already knows this stuff. "But we're glad to have the graduates, too, because this is the place for them to share all their knowledge and wisdom with others."

- *The Student.* This is the attentive, hardworking, perfect participant who wants to hear what you have to say. He is eager to learn and share and, like a sponge, ready to absorb all he can to help him be more effective personally and professionally. "We always welcome the students!"

Some audiences represent a combination of these traits—but most fit nicely into one of the categories. Familiarizing yourself with these categories will help you prepare a thorough audience analysis and assist you in delivering your speech.

Before I give a speech, through my preprogram survey, I can usually identify if there will be one or more audience members who have expertise on my topic. I try to contact them before the program and ask if I can use an example from their experience to help illustrate my points. I tell the "graduate" I appreciate the help and acknowledge his or her expertise during my presentation. What I find is that the "graduate" now becomes my ally and adds another element of interest to my presentation. During the presentation, I poll the audience to find out if any participants have expertise in my topic and invite them to share their knowledge, too. For example, quite often I have senior vice presidents, vice presidents, and middle management attend my seminars. Most of these professionals attend to make sure the other participants, their employees, are getting the skills they need. Some also attend to fine-tune their own public speaking skills. Some are already excellent speakers who are looking to go further in their careers and want to pick my brain and see what I do. Knowing that these individuals are more experienced, I make every attempt to include them in exercises and solicit their input during the seminar.

Speaking to Groups: Large and Small

When speaking to an audience, also take the size into consideration. You may need to make adjustments and adapt your speaking style, especially your gestures, to the size of the audience and the room. I have spoken to groups as small as one and as large as six thousand! Can you imagine what it feels like speaking to six thousand people? If this thought still scares you, go back and review my tips on speech anxiety in Day 1.

If the room is small enough, for example, you may not need a microphone, and it may be necessary for you to deemphasize your gestures a little so people can focus on your words. In smaller groups you may want to keep your gestures closer to your body, above the waist, and below the shoulders. You want to use the same natural gestures with smaller groups as with large ones, such as gestures with your arms, legs, or entire body, except that the degree of motion needs to be smaller.

With a larger audience, you may need to exaggerate those same gestures to make an impact. If the group is large enough, it makes sense to gesture above your head or way out from your body. The only exception to this is if the arena or auditorium is so large that you are projected on a large screen. Since your image is being projected, you don't need to make your gestures larger than normal. Also, speaking to a group of more than fifty people requires a microphone and a good sound system. Many professional speakers use wireless microphones with all the appropriate jacks to fit into any sound system. Here's another tip: Engaging a large audience in a question and answer period may not be appropriate; encourage audience participants to come up and speak to you individually after the program.

Types of Speeches

There are many types of speeches you may be asked to give in your professional and personal life. I will discuss and analyze each type of speech in Days 6 to 10. Your audience analysis can help you make the best speech possible. Consider tailoring your surveys to focus on questions related to your type of speech. For example, if you are giving a tribute speech, include a survey question or two about what audience members feel or remember most strongly about the person being celebrated.

- The informative speech
- The demonstration speech
- The persuasive speech
- The ceremonial speech or tribute speech
- The impromptu or extemporaneous speech

The Informative Speech

The informative speech teaches a piece of information to the audience. You need to tell the audience why the information is useful and valuable. For example:

- A tour guide explaining the history of ancient ruins
- A computer programmer explaining the benefits and capabilities of a new kind of software
- A doctor explaining the latest treatment for Alzheimer's disease

The Demonstration Speech

A demonstration speech is similar to an informative speech, except you tell the audience how to do something.

Key words to differentiate between demonstration and informative speeches is "how to." For example:

- A ski instructor demonstrating how to maneuver on your skis
- A computer programmer teaching a company division how to operate a new e-mail system
- A sales associate teaching new employees how to catalog merchandise

The Persuasive Speech

In a persuasive speech you are persuading the audience to make a change, such as how they think about conflict, or get the audience to do something they do not do now. For example:

- A lawyer trying to convince a jury
- A public relations executive trying to persuade a client to expand its marketing program or change its logo or slogan
- A salesman trying to persuade a customer to buy one model of a particular car over another

The Ceremonial Speech

In a ceremonial speech, you acknowledge or honor a person or organization for something he or she has accomplished. For example:

- Presenting an award to an association member
- Dedicating the new town library
- Acting as master of ceremonies for an event

The Impromptu or Extemporaneous Speech

There may be situations when you are called upon to address a group of people with no warning, whether it's in class, work, or social situations. For example:

- Being invited to the head table at a meeting and asked to say a few words about the upcoming fund-raiser
- Feeling the need to agree with or rebut something that was said at a town council meeting
- Finding yourself the guest of honor at a surprise birthday party, with the crowd yelling, "Speech, speech!"

Lessons from Mom: Do Your Homework

I do not think anyone will ever forget their mother saying, "Did you do your homework?" just as you were running out the door to go hang out with your friends. Today, before I give a speech, I can still recall my mother saying those words to me. Right now you may be the parent who is asking that of your own kids. As students you learned how important it was for you to do your homework for the next day's class. I can recall those few times when I did not do all my homework and I walked into class and the teacher decided to surprise us with a pop quiz based on our homework. That's when I remembered my mother asking, "Did you do your homework, Lenny?"

Public speaking is no different. If you do not "do your homework" and prepare yourself properly, your speech or presentation may flunk the test. Part of your responsibility as a speaker is being prepared for your presentations by doing your homework. A key aspect of your homework, as a speaker, includes gathering information about your audience and their needs. A well-prepared speech given to the wrong audience or not tailored to an audience can have the same effect as a poorly prepared speech given to the correct audience—both can fail miserably. It is critical that your preparation include audience analysis. The more you know and understand about your audience, the better you can prepare your speech to meet their needs.

Tip of the Day

To guarantee your audience walks away remembering the important points from your presentation, give a review or summary at the end of it. One effective strategy is to refer to the original agenda and ask the audience to tell you what they learned about each point. Have them do this as a group and write down the points as they tell you. You watch—it will become a contest among them, but a fun one. This process allows you to drive your point home effectively.

If I use an overhead projector, I face the audience as I write on the transparency. If I use a flip chart, I stand off to the side so I don't block the chart and write their responses. That's very important: Never speak with your back to the audience. Also, do not speak when you are writing the responses. Write the information down, face the audience, and then continue speaking. Ask the audience to provide you with the top two best ideas they learned from each section of your presentation. Review these ideas against the objectives you provided at the start of your presentation. When the audience sees that you met all their objectives, you have shown that you have delivered what you promised.

In Day 4 I discuss creative strategies you can use to remember speech material. I examine the four most common methods and analyze the pros and cons of each.

Day 4

Remembering What You Have to Say

Remembering speech and presentation material can be very intimidating, even for the most seasoned professional. But don't worry, there are many methods you can use to help you remember material—all of them will help build your confidence in public speaking.

Techniques for Remembering Speech Material

The four most common methods of remembering speech and presentation material are the following:

1. Memorizing
2. Reading from complete text
3. Using notes
4. Using visual aids

Let's take a look at each of these in more detail, including the pros and cons. You will notice that some of the tips apply to all the methods; that's okay, it only emphasizes their importance.

Memorizing

Perhaps the most difficult of the four methods, memorizing is the technique many novice speakers start off with, because they are under the impression that this is how all speeches are prepared and delivered. I actually do not recommend memorizing your speech: Although the outcome can be very effective, memorizing a speech word for word and then delivering it requires a lot of preparation and practice. First you must write or type out the speech. Since most people do not write the way they speak, this creates an immediate problem. For example, the use of gestures and proper voice inflection in conjunction with a memorized speech tends to be very flat and unengaging. Even if you are successful in using gestures and a lively tone of voice, it's entirely possible that you will forget portions of your speech. Listening to thousands of speeches over my career, I have watched even the most polished speakers forget their words halfway through. With memorizing, mental blocks are inevitable, and it is not a question of "Will you forget?" but "when you will forget?" Can you memorize a speech? Yes. Should you memorize a speech? I don't recommend it. Speakers who rely strictly on memorization are setting themselves up for failure.

Another risk factor with memorized speeches is that the spontaneity is gone—you sound stilted. What tends to happen is that the delivery is too rapid (usually owing to nerves). Your concentration is on getting the words out, not the ideas, and you tend to come across as too formal, like a written essay. Worst of all, if your mind goes blank and you make a mistake, the flow of your speech is interrupted. You get flustered, your confidence is shot, and in most cases it's just not appropriate to start over.

Reading from Complete Text

Most people dislike listening to someone read a speech or presentation, even if the speaker makes a concerted effort to maintain eye contact with the audience. Your audience is just likely to end up saying, "If all he was going to do was read his speech, I could have read it myself." I'm sure each of you has experienced the monotone drone of a read speech while attending a conference. Following are the reasons I believe people read speeches poorly:

- The speaker loses normal voice inflection because he loses touch with the ideas behind the words. Listen for pauses. Natural speech is filled with pauses; unnatural speech is not.
- The text being read is usually not written in the manner and style of spoken language. Too often speakers write their speeches in "business language" that is often very difficult to read, much less listen to.
- The speaker achieves little or no eye contact. Any eye contact is with the manuscript and not with the audience. To maintain eye contact with the audience and read text effectively takes a lot of practice. You have to take in several lines at a time and keep your place. You are very likely to find yourself losing your place every time you look up to speak to the audience.

Don't get me wrong, there are times when speeches must be read. For example, it is often necessary to read policy statements or company announcements. To avoid mistakes when some element of a speech must be communicated word for word, the speaker reads directly from written text. There are also occasions when a speech must be timed down to the second, as in a debate. In my opinion, reading a speech well is actually more difficult than speaking extemporaneously. Although people hear all the time that they should not read their speech, most feel this is the only way they can actually give one. For those of you who feel compelled to read your speech, I'll help you at least sound better when you do.

If reading is absolutely necessary, here are some suggestions to make your reading sound more professional.

- **Pay attention to your voice inflection.** To sound natural you need to rehearse often, checking yourself for pauses. Ask yourself if your written words sound the way you would speak them. Tape yourself and listen to your own voice. Note where changes need to be made with your voice inflection. Try not to overinflect your voice or it will become distracting to your audience.
- **Say the words out loud.** As you're practicing your speech, read it out loud several times so you can hear your tone and voice inflection. The more you practice reading, the more comfortable and familiar with the words you become. Using this approach makes it easier to read your speech and for the audience to listen to it.
- **Annotate your text.** Give yourself cues for emphasis in the margin of your text. For example, numbers are the easiest target words to say slowly and with emphasis. You want to emphasize each syllable of any number word. For example, if you have the word *fifty* in your speech, and it appears as 50, make a note in the margin, so you say "fif-ty" when you get to it.
- **Use gestures.** Many speakers are so busy making sure they read the text correctly, they fail to communicate

effectively with their body. One strategy is to double-space your typed text. This leaves room for you to jot down notes and cues about which words to emphasize and gestures to accompany certain sentences, points, or key messages. You need to practice the annotated text of the speech so you can correctly read it and identify cues for your gestures so they come across naturally. This takes practice. Professionals do this very effectively to the point where you almost don't know they are reading. Again, don't overgesture or it can draw your audience away from listening to your message.

- **Videotape yourself.** I still videotape my speeches and presentations, especially those I deliver for the first time. I recommend you sit down with a pen and paper in your hand and take notes as you watch your video. Watch the video several times, each time taking notes on different things you see. Here is the process I use to review my videotapes:
    - **Review 1.** Watch the entire tape (alone) without being too critical. Watch the tape as an audience might for the first time.
    - **Review 2.** Darken the picture or turn your back to the television so you cannot see yourself but you can hear your voice. Record on your notepad things you liked and disliked about your voice; for example, listen to how you phrase your words and the inflection in your voice.
    - **Review 3.** Turn down the sound and just watch yourself. Watch how you use your hands, your facial expressions, or any nervous habits or distracting mannerisms. Again, record the things you want to change, improve, or eliminate. At the same time,

note any gestures you feel work well and look natural.

- **Review 4.** Watch the tape again with the volume turned up and take more notes. See if there are any areas you missed during earlier reviews.
- **Review 5.** Have someone else watch the tape who will be honest and objective, such as your spouse, child, friend, and so on. As they watch the video, look at their reactions to your speech and then ask them, after the tape is done, to tell you what they liked and disliked. Having watched your own video four times prior, you are prepared to deal with any feedback, even negative.

This review process is probably the single best technique you can use to help you learn, improve, and modify how you deliver a speech or presentation.

Physically Prepare Your Speech

Here are three tips to help you physically prepare your speech so you don't sound as though you are reading it to the audience.

- **Write the way you speak.** As I said earlier, people who read speeches have little or no eye contact with the audience. To avoid this, write in the voice you use when talking to family and friends. Then type your speech using upper- and lowercase letters, which are much easier to read than all caps (capital letters). TYPING EVERYTHING IN UPPERCASE AS I HAVE DONE HERE MAKES TEXT MUCH MORE DIFFICULT TO READ.

- **Keep paragraphs short and succinct.** Start a new paragraph every couple of sentences, the way you often see in newspaper articles. Some people go so far as alternating the text color for each paragraph. Also, don't have any sentence or paragraph begin on one page and run over to the next. Start each page with a new paragraph. This allows you to pause as you move to the next page.
- **Fasten pages together.** Fasten your pages with a paper clip, not a staple, and remove it before you begin. Number each page. You would be amazed how many people have dropped their unnumbered speech notes. Disaster! Keep in mind that you will have to handle these pages during your speech, and you want to do this as smoothly and quietly as you can. During your pauses, slowly slide the page you have just finished to one side and continue with the text on the next page. Do not pick up the page and place it behind the previous page or turn the page over. Your audience will see you do it, and it brings attention to the fact that you are reading your speech.

With a lot of practice and careful preparation, you can be successful at speech reading.

Using Notes

Notes capture the major sections and main points of each section. I recommend using either note or index cards. This is the most common way to remember speech material. Using notes has more advantages than reading because you use your normal voice inflection and make more effective eye contact with your audience. Here are suggestions to consider if you decide to use notes.

- **Keep it brief.** Don't write out whole paragraphs of text. Put only a few key words or phrases on each card, just enough to jog your memory. Also put only one or two ideas on each card, and print large and neatly so your notes are easy to read.
- **Remember to number your note cards!** Just in case you drop them.
- **Include quotes, statistics, and lists.** Don't include whole paragraphs of text.
- **Leave your notes on the lectern or table as you're speaking and move away occasionally.** Don't be afraid to move away from your notes and get out of your comfort zone. Too many speakers use the lectern to hide behind, and this restricts the use of your body. If the notes are in your hand, you won't gesture as often.
- **Practice using your note cards.** Practice helps you analyze your note cards. For example, if you find yourself reading from your note cards too much, reduce the amount of written text on your cards.
- **Use pictures and maps.** You don't have to use just words on your note cards. Pictures and maps help you visualize the key points of your speech. In some cases it's best to draw a sketch or diagram on your note cards. Sometimes a simple drawing is all you need to jog your memory. Also use mental pictures to tell a story in your mind. This takes creativity, but it's worth the effort. For example, picture in your mind the events as they unfold. As you relive the story, whether it's true or fictional, it's easier to visualize your speech as a story rather than a group of words written in a certain order.

Using Visual Aids

Simple visual aids effectively serve as headings or subheadings on your topic and allow your audience to visually see what you are discussing. Create meaningful headings, and practice using only these headings as your cues. This takes time to master, but practicing helps you internalize your speech. For example, one visual aid might read, "How to structure a presentation." Then you can speak extemporaneously from what you know. If you have properly prepared your speech, you can speak in a conversational manner. When I give a presentation I use slides. Here is an example of a slide I use when giving a seminar entitled "How to Overcome Speaking Anxiety in Meetings and Presentations."

- Symptoms of Speaking Anxiety

  —Anxiety.

  —Sweaty palms.

  —Nervousness.

- Mental Techniques to Reduce Speaking Anxiety

  —Prepare and rehearse.

  —Use positive self-talk.

  —Be natural, but enthusiastic.

- Physical Techniques to Reduce Speaking Anxiety

  —Take a brisk walk before you speak.

  —Use deep breathing exercises.

  —Don't sit with your legs crossed.

Choosing the right visual aid for your presentation is as important as its design. Following are tips to consider when using visual aids and notes:

- **Use the KISS method.** This is an acronym for "Keep it short and simple." Use no more than one idea per visual aid. Use no more than six or seven lines per visual aid and no more than six or seven words per line.
- **Use descriptive titles.** The title of each visual aid should be a simple summary of what is on the visual aid. A clear title helps grab the attention of the audience and helps you and the audience remember your main message for that particular visual aid.
- **Use the same design for each of your visuals.** Use the same color, text size, and font type. The idea is to be visually and stylistically consistent.
- **Make copies of your handouts.** Make sure you bring enough for everyone, and always have extras. I recommend keeping a copy of your handouts for two reasons. First, you have a copy to refer to during your presentation. Also, if you are using an overhead projector and it breaks or the bulb burns out and you don't have a replacement, you can refer to your handouts without stopping the flow of your speech. In addition, I keep an original copy of my handouts, one without notations written on them, in case I need to make any last minute copies for workshop participants.
- **Proofread your visual aids.** Proofread for typos and grammatical errors. Then proof again. Then have someone else proofread them. It is amazing how you can review your own visual aids and skip right over the same misspelled word each time. Having others proofread your slides helps you find other mistakes. Don't assume that the spell checker on your word processor will catch all the errors. For example, if you type "cat" when you meant "chat," your spell checker won't catch that error since "cat" is a word.

Keep in mind, your visual aids are not limited to words. They can also contain diagrams, drawings, pictures, or even objects.

Regardless of the method you choose for remembering material, nothing helps you more than proper planning, preparation, and practice.

Positive Performance: The Most Creative Ideas for Presenting Material

As you think about developing presentation material, consider the different ways you've seen presentations delivered. For example, if a presenter pulls out a one-inch-high stack of overhead transparencies, you're likely to say to yourself, This is going to be boring. No one said you couldn't be entertaining while giving a speech or presentation.

Your audience needs to be an intricate part of your presentation. Give them something to do during your presentation other than just listen. Be creative. Don't restrict yourself to using only overhead transparencies or slides. Try new things.

The Northwestern School of Speech reports that the attention span of an audience is approximately nine seconds. The attention is the highest at the beginning and at the end of the presentation. What this means is that you have a free ride during the first few minutes; however, if you blow the first few minutes, you've lost them for the remaining time. Remember, the audience is always checking you out and asking themselves, Is this going to be worth listening to? or I wish I'd sat in the back near the door so I could sneak out. The solution? Spice up your presentation every six to eight minutes. Add elements to keep it alive, exciting, and interesting. Here are ways to make your presentation come alive.

- **Use humor.** In the next section I provide some Web sites that I recommend as resources for polishing speaking skills; note the last one, which deals with humor. Also, trust your instincts and free yourself up to use your own natural sense of humor in appropriate places.
- **Use information and quotes from newspaper and magazine articles.** Find articles that relate to your topic—a human interest story, research results, or an article about the latest industry issue or trend—and incorporate them into your presentation.
- **Incorporate questions during your presentation.** Asking open-ended questions encourages your audience to think. I phrase most of my questions with the five *w*'s: who, what, when, where, and why. Here are two example questions I've asked many times in my seminars: "How many of you think speaking to a large group of people is more difficult than speaking to a small, intimate group?" and "What kinds of symptoms have you experienced when you're nervous about speaking to a group?" These questions can be planned ahead and asked of the group or directed to an individual.
- **Use analogies. Include any of your "war stories" as part of your presentation.** People love hearing stories, but make sure the stories illustrate a point and are not there just to fill the time slot. For example, when I gave my motivational speech to the group at the Mt. Snow ski resort in New England (see Day 3), I compared the challenges of preparing a presentation to the challenges of skiing down a mountain, emphasizing how sometimes you fall, but you force yourself to get back up and try again.

Let me share a "war story" I tell in my workshops when I discuss the importance of knowing the size of your audience.

When I was still an engineer I was asked by a colleague to speak at an engineering conference for five hundred people at the Grand Ole Opry Hotel in Nashville, Tennessee. After agreeing, I asked him not to schedule my presentation on the first day because I would be traveling. When I arrived at the hotel I learned I was scheduled as the second to last speaker on the final day of the three-day conference. To make matters worse, I was scheduled right after lunch. If any of you have spoken at conferences, you know that this is not a premium speaking spot because people are tired and may be feeling sleepy from eating a big meal.

On the day of the presentation I was prepared, psyched, and pumped. Ten minutes before my presentation one gentleman arrived and sat in the twentieth row. Five minutes before my speech, another gentleman arrived and said, "Hi, my name is Rob, and I'm the session chairman for this segment of the conference. Are you ready to begin?" There I was, thinking that I was getting ready to give a presentation to five hundred people. I later learned that many of the attendees had an early tee time for the golf course.

Like all good speakers, I started on time, and at the end of my presentation I said to the gentleman in the twentieth row, "I really appreciate your showing up and listening to my presentation." What he said next to me, I will never forget: "That's okay, I'm next!"

Whenever I think about my audience analysis and I ask people what they would find most difficult, speaking to a large or small group of people, I always think of that day. Would you rather address a crowded room or one person?

Internet Resources That Help Your Presentation Shine

There's no doubt about it—the Internet is an integral part of our lives. I've had a Web site since 1996, and it's a crucial part of my business and marketing efforts. Here is a list of articles and tips that will help you polish your speaking skills. Take some time to visit these sites. This list is not comprehensive, but rather includes sites I believe offer the most valuable information.

- **www.ljlseminars.com/monthtip.htm.** A collection of tips on various topics related to public speaking and presentation skills. This site is updated frequently (I know because it's mine!). I also provide a free monthly e-zine titled *Simply Speaking,* which is e-mailed to over nineteen thousand subscribers each month.
- **www.performanceanxiety.com.** This is the site of the Spotlight LLC (limited liability corporation), a company owned and run by Janet Esposito. Esposito's company is devoted to creating products and services to help people who suffer from public speaking performance anxiety.
- **www.abacon.com/pubspeak.** This site contains five modules concerning the process of public speaking: assessing, analyzing, researching, organizing, and delivering your speech.
- **www.greatvoice.com.** Susan Berkley is recognized as one of the nation's top female voice-over artists; her voice has sold millions of dollars' worth of speaking products and services on TV and radio commercials. In addition, Susan's voice is the telephone voice of many Fortune 500 companies' greeting systems. Susan is also

the author of the book *Speak to Influence—How to Unlock the Hidden Power of Your Voice.*

- **www.ukans.edu/~sypherh/bc/relinks.html.** This site, called Virtual Presentation Assistant (from the University of Kansas), provides links to other sites useful to basic course directors, teaching assistants, and students—much of the information is also relevant to professional or amateur speakers. It includes links to on-line writing centers, journals, instructional Web research, and university teaching centers.
- **www.govst.edu/commcentral/inter.htm.** Provides links to dozens of other sites with useful information on improving communication with people from various cultures and countries.
- **www.presentersuniversity.com.** This is a free on-line resource that provides valuable, easy-to-use information (tips, tools, and training) to help you develop effective multimedia presentations.
- **www.presentingsolutions.com/effectivepresentations.html.** This site sells equipment such as film recorders and projectors for great presentations—it's also worthwhile if you are looking for a short refresher course on presenting.
- **www.sayitbetter.com.** Kare Anderson is a behavioral futurist who speaks and writes about what she calls "Say It Better" methods of thoughtful communication, conflict resolution and outreach, and multisensory techniques to create more memorable speaking experiences.
- **www.antion.com.** Tom Antion, a colleague of mine, is an internationally acclaimed expert in the field of high-impact techniques for using humor.

Here are some additional Web sites you will find useful:

- Public Speaker Magazine: www.speakup.co.uk
- The Speaking Connection: www.speakingconnection.com
- Presentations Magazine: www.presentations.com

Location, Location: How the Setting of Your Speech Affects Your Delivery

The location where you deliver your speech can enhance or interfere with the effectiveness of your presentation. It is very important to find out what the facilities look like before you speak. It is always best, if possible, to visit in advance the location and room where you will be speaking. If you can't visit beforehand, find out the room layout from the meeting planner, coordinator, or hotel staff. When I make arrangements for my public seminars, I always contact the meeting planner, person in charge of the seminar, or hotel staff and send a sketch of how I want the room laid out. For example, the sketch shows how I want the tables set up (such as classroom style or dinner style) and where I'll be addressing the audience. Here are some points you may want to address with the meeting planner or convention hall or hotel staff:

1. Room location
2. Room size
3. Room layout
4. Chair and table arrangements
5. Door and window locations
6. Lighting

7. Signage: directing the participants to the room location
8. Hotel background music
9. Room temperature controls
10. Other functions taking place in the hotel or convention center during your seminar (find out what's going on in the room next door)
11. Food arrangements
12. Audiovisual requirements
13. Phone lines
14. Storage and security for seminar equipment

Let's take a moment to look more closely at each of these factors for creating a professional speaking environment.

Room Location

Quite often you won't have much control over the room location unless you're presenting in your own company. If possible, visit the conference rooms available to you and decide which room is appropriate for your presentation.

- As I said, prepare a diagram of how you want the room set up and mail or fax a copy of it to the corporation or facility where you'll be speaking.
- Call the staff member in charge of the seminar and discuss your needs; see if you can make an on-site visit.
- Check parking and fees involved, if applicable. Inform attendees ahead of time, by including a note or flyer in preconference mailings.
- Send attendees the name and address of the hotel or conference center and the room name or number in which the presentation is being given.

- Send attendees a detailed map showing the exact location and directions.

Room Size

The size of the room you will need depends on the number of people attending your seminar or meeting. Obviously the room size and setup is different for ten people than for several hundred.

The room size should provide adequate space for you, your visual aids, your equipment, and your participants. There is nothing worse than being crammed into a room the size of a closet. At the same time, you don't want to feel you are in an auditorium unless you need the larger room to accommodate your group. Here are some more tips.

- Arrive early. I like to arrive at least two hours before a speaking engagement. When I travel, I ask to see the room the evening before, if possible. This allows me to make any last minute adjustments with my presentation.
- If I am one of many speakers on a program or a multiday conference, I arrive early and sit in the room I will be speaking in to get a feel for it.

Room Layout

The layout of the room has a tremendous effect on the success of your meeting or seminar. Many hotel staff are not aware of the preferred room layout style required by speakers. A majority of hotels set the rooms in one of two ways:

1. Auditorium or theater style
2. Dinner style

On the following pages I give setup preferences I use at my speaking engagements and a pro and con for each one. The four common room setups are

1. classroom style;
2. U-shaped workshop style;
3. theater style or lecture style;
4. dinner style.

Classroom Style

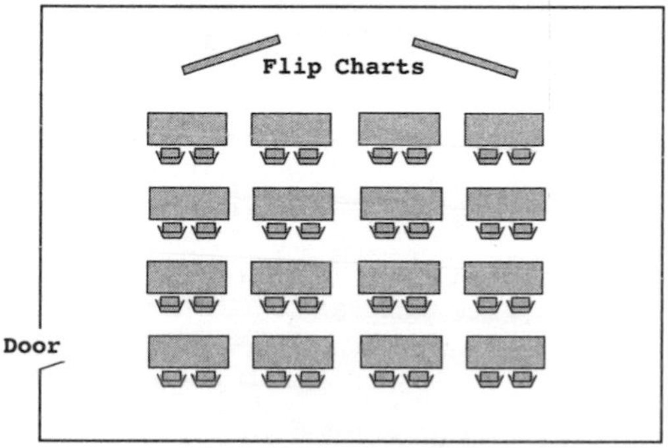

Poor Arrangement

Reason: The seats and tables are arranged in linear rows, and the setup doesn't allow participants to make easy eye contact.

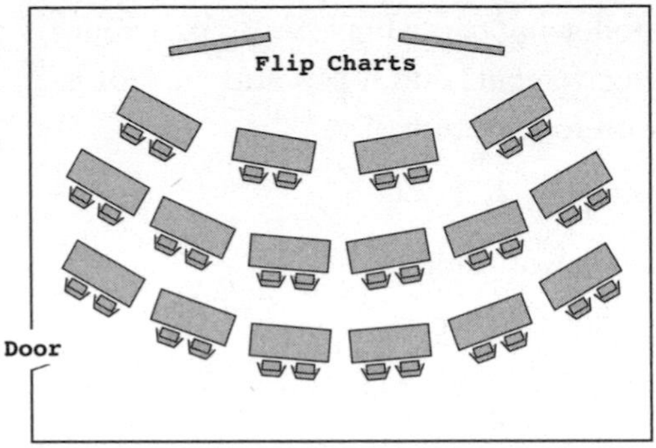

Better Arrangement

Reason: This arrangement allows the participants to see one another more easily and encourages more interaction and participation.

U-shaped Style

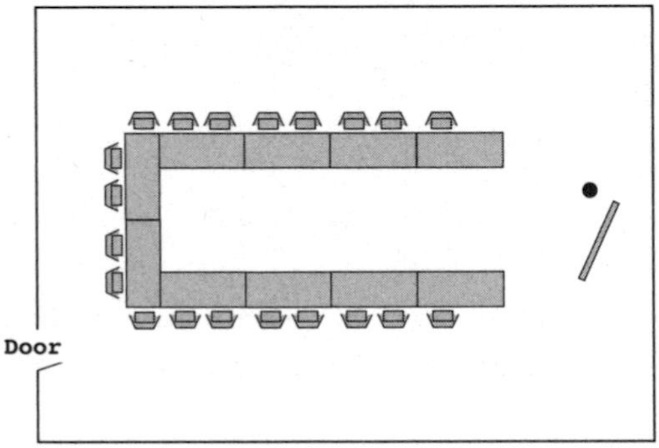

Poor Arrangement

Reason: This arrangement doesn't allow the presenter, indicated by the small black dot, to be close enough to his or her audience.

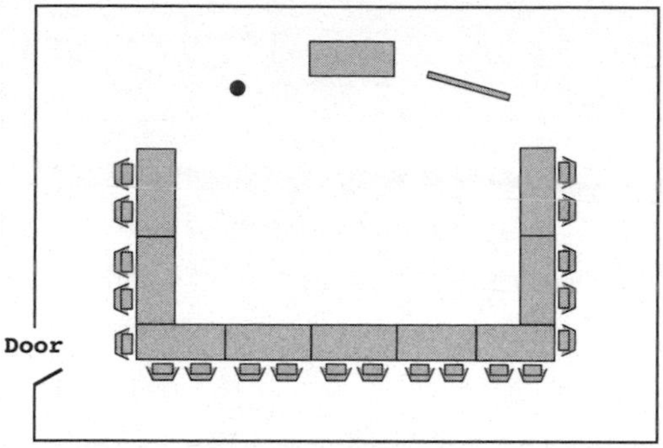

Better Arrangement

Reason: This arrangement allows the presenter, indicated by the small black dot, to be closer to his or her audience, giving the presentation a more comfortable atmosphere.

Theater or Lecture Style

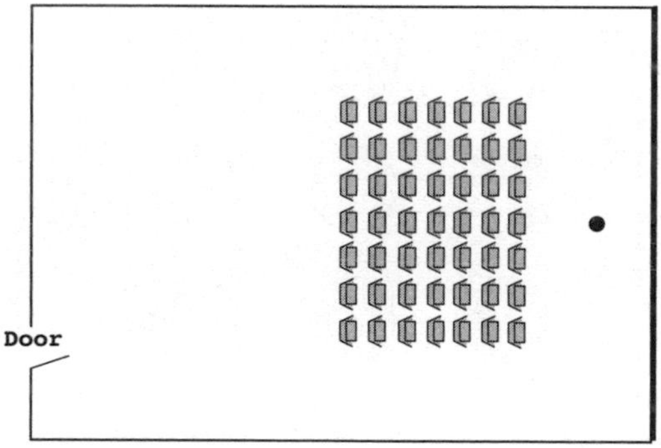

Poor Arrangement

Reason: Participants are too crammed together and far away from the presenter.

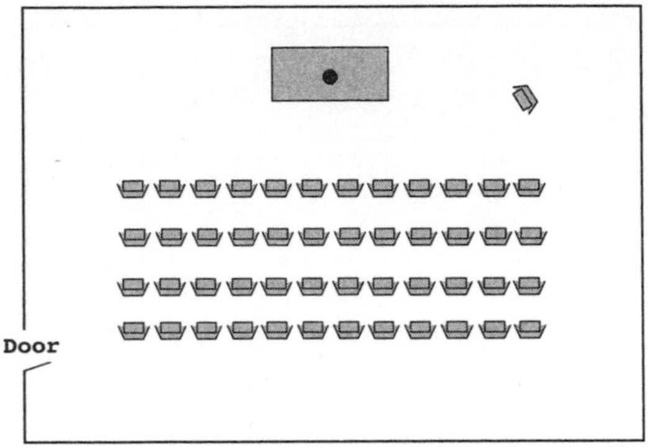

Better Arrangement

Reason: This setup places the speaker closer to the audience and gives the audience more room between seats.

Dinner Style

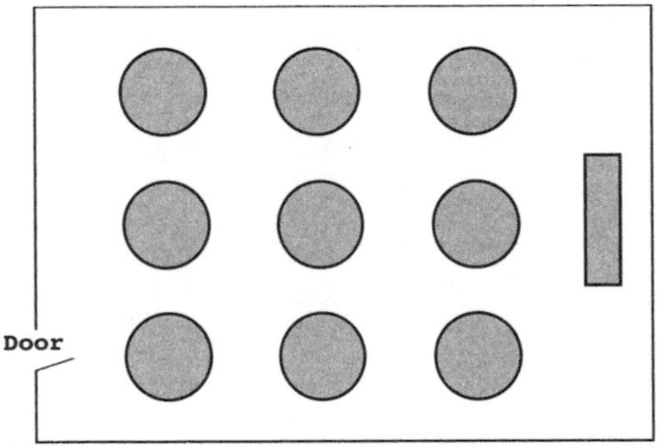

Poor Arrangement

Reason: Tables are set up in perfect rows and will obstruct the audience's view of the speaker.

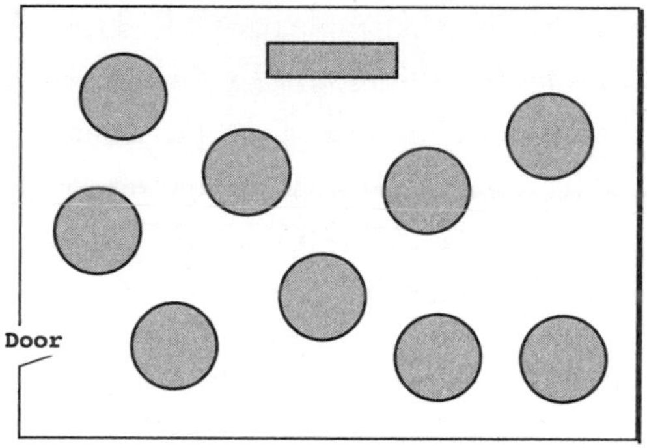

Better Arrangement

Reason: This setup staggers the tables and prevents blocking the participants' view of the speaker and head table.

Chair and Table Arrangements

- Arrange the chairs in advance with as few rows as possible. Do not have more tables and chairs set up than you need. Most people tend to sit in the back rows of the room and avoid the front row at all costs because they fear being picked on during the presentation to answer a question or participate in a demonstration.
- Some speakers put out fewer chairs than they need and leave extras stacked in the back of the room, creating the impression of a full seminar or workshop.
- Tape Reserved signs on the back few rows of chairs. This forces the attendees to sit closer to the front.
- Provide tables if possible. This gives people a more comfortable place to write.
- Don't cram too many chairs behind seminar tables. Most hotel tables seat three people comfortably, but I

prefer to sit only two people per table. This accomplishes two things: first, it gives my seminar participants more room; and second, it forces you to use more tables, creating a fuller seminar room.

- Provide soft, comfortable chairs if you are giving an all-day or multiday program.
- Leave plenty of room between tables and chairs to allow people to move freely around the room. This is especially important if you are providing refreshments during the seminar.

Door and Window Locations

Arrange the chairs and tables so the doors are at the back of the room, allowing people to arrive and sit down quickly without interrupting you.

- Serve refreshments near the back of the room, where most people congregate during breaks and can easily come and go.
- Set up a table with your speaking products (if you have them) in the back. For example, I bring copies of my books, videotapes, and audiotapes for participants. In addition, I bring my brochures, product catalogs, and promotional materials to my speaking engagements. If possible, I set up a table in a location where participants enter and exit the room. This encourages them to stop and peruse what I have to offer.

Windows are an important part of the room layout. Obviously you have no control of the window location. However, if you believe the windows are a distraction:

- See if a room without windows is available; if not, close the curtains or blinds.

Lighting

Proper lighting plays a key role in your presentation. If the lights are too dim, it could put the participants to sleep. If the lights are too bright, it could bother their eyes and make it hard to see visual aids, especially overhead transparencies and slides.

- Check lighting prior to your meeting or seminar.
- Ask yourself if it's bright enough for everyone to see.
- Make sure you know where the light controls are located and how to use them. For example, if you're using an overhead projector or slide carousel, you'll need to adjust the lights.
- Label the switches to remind you what part of the room each controls, such as overhead, back, or front.
- Never put the room in complete darkness.
- If the room has lamps, turn them off so your audience won't be distracted. It may not be necessary to turn off every lamp. Do what you believe will make the room comfortable for your presentation and audience.
- See if it's possible to use a spotlight, or bring in additional lighting if the room is too dark for your liking.

Signage

If your attendees can't find you or get lost finding you throughout the hotel conference area or convention hall, they'll be in a foul mood even before you start your presentation.

- Place several signs clearly indicating the room location. This helps if the room is located in a separate wing of the building.
- Ask the front desk or welcoming table staff to give attendees directions to the meeting location.

Hotel Background Music

Music can be distracting during a presentation unless it's part of your program. If you find the room has music:

- Find out how to turn it off. Some hotels do not have individual room controls, and you don't want to compete with the music, so ask at the front desk or speak to the person in charge. Some rooms have controls where you can turn off the music yourself.
- Use either royalty-free music where you don't have to pay royalties (a fee) to the producer or musical artist, or use music you received permission to play. Several companies on the Internet offer royalty-free music. Occasionally I use lively music when the guests first arrive. I play softer, more soothing music during the breaks. However, the music I choose isn't tied in to my presentation.

Room Temperature Controls

It's important that the room be comfortable for you and your attendees.

- Find out from the hotel or convention hall how to control the room temperature. Many hotel rooms or convention halls have thermostats, but many times these have a Plexiglas cover and are locked.

- Ask if the lock can be removed during your seminar.
- Get a name and number to reach the hotel personnel or convention hall manager if you are not permitted to control the temperature.

Other Functions at the Same Location

Giving a speech is difficult enough. The last thing you need to worry about is the class reunion with a disc jockey next door.

- Find out if any other functions are happening simultaneously with your seminar (such as a wedding).
- If this is the case, ask if you can move your function to another room. If this happens at the last minute, ask for the hotel staff's help in preparing appropriate signage to direct attendees to the new room. This scenario has occurred only a few times in my professional speaking career. For example, if I learn a wedding is next door and I can't change my room, I try to get a time frame from someone involved in the wedding reception. I can find out when the "loud" portions of the wedding are occurring, such as introducing the bridal party and cutting the cake, so I'm not competing with the noise.

Food Arrangements

If you are planning to have food served as part of your function:

- Inform the conference director of your intent to serve food. Many hotels give you a better room rate if they know you are serving food.
- In the morning provide coffee, tea, juice, pastry, and fresh fruit. Many people need their coffee and may have headaches (or just become annoyed) by midmorning if you don't offer it. Provide soft drinks and light snacks for afternoon seminars, and always have ice water and mints available.
- Ask the hotel or convention hall staff if you and your attendees can preorder from a menu sheet if you are not serving a set menu. Include the menu sheet in your meeting packet, so attendees can fill it out upon arrival at the seminar. Provide a box to put the forms in, and make sure whoever's greeting attendees lets them know they need to fill this out.
- Arrange to have someone pick up the food if you are not ordering from the location's catering facility.
- If you are not providing refreshments, allow the group enough time if they have to go out for lunch.
- Provide a list for your participants of local restaurants near the hotel or convention hall.

Audiovisual Requirements

It's always a good idea to make sure that all your audiovisual requirements are arranged well ahead of time. Don't assume that just because you asked or sent your requirements in writing that every detail will be taken care of to your satisfaction.

- Arrive early and check that you have everything you need.

- Bring your own equipment if you are speaking locally. This guarantees you will have everything you need.
- Test your audiovisuals. Plug in the slide projector and make sure it's working. Test your slide carousel to make sure your slides will advance.

Phone Lines

Having the proper phone connections is crucial if your seminar involves using a modem. I require phone lines when I'm doing Internet marketing seminars.

- Arrange for phone lines when you book the room. Take into consideration that not every room in the hotel or convention center is equipped with phone jacks.
- If the room has a phone and it's not part of your seminar, turn off the ringer so you and your attendees aren't distracted by a ringing telephone.

Storage and Security for Seminar Equipment

Depending on the seminar topic, I sometimes require the use of a computer, overhead projector, slide carousel, spotlight, or microphone. Here are some tips on the best ways to store your equipment at your speaking location.

- Make sure you have arranged well in advance, preferably when you book the room, for the proper storage of your equipment.
- Make sure you have access to the room if it's locked. I recommend getting a key from the appropriate personnel so you can enter and exit the room as you please.

Tip of the Day

As your presentation skills improve, you may find yourself being asked to give a speech or say a few words about an associate, friend, or family member at a special event or occasion. Often you don't have time to prepare. Following are tips I used to give a spontaneous speech following a dance recital at which my daughter received her first dance trophy.

I remember when Kelly first began to dance and perform; she was only two. During her years as a dancer, we would stop for ice cream after each recital to celebrate what a great job she did. At most recitals, those dancers who have performed for five or more years are usually presented with a trophy to acknowledge their accomplishment. When Kelly received her first trophy we again went out for ice cream and invited the group who came to see Kelly to join us. On this occasion I gave a short speech about what a great job she did and how proud she made her family. This short speech had only a few main points:

- Thank the people who attended the recital for showing Kelly their support.
- Congratulate Kelly for doing a great job.
- Acknowledge the fact that she received an award.

I then closed by saying, "Let's dig in."

So the next time you have an opportunity to give a speech to celebrate an achievement, you can at least do the following even if you don't have time to prepare:

- Decide how you want to begin the speech. In my example, I thanked people for coming.

- Acknowledge the person receiving the achievement. Make sure you mention the name of the achievement or award and what it means.
- Include a personal story about the person being honored—keep it fun and upbeat.

In Day 5 I will discuss my favorite aspect of speaking and presentation skills—gestures. The ability to gesture effectively, often referred to as "nonverbal communication," is crucial to your success as a public speaker.

Day 5

Say It with Style

Body Language and Voice

Research has demonstrated that over half of all human communication takes place on the nonverbal level. When you speak before a group, your listeners base their judgment of you and your message on what they see as well as on what they hear.

Your body is an effective tool for adding emphasis and clarity to your words. It's also your most powerful instrument for convincing an audience of your sincerity, earnestness, and enthusiasm. However, if your physical actions don't agree with your verbal message, your body can defeat your words. Remember the following credo:

Effective speech delivery involves the whole person.

Positive Performance: Letting Your Body Mirror Your Message

You can learn to use your entire body as an instrument of speech. As the speaker, you are the most important visual aid for your audience. Here are reasons you are important:

1. You don't have to darken the room to be seen.
2. You don't burn out.
3. You don't jam up.
4. You don't break.
5. You aren't one-dimensional.
6. You don't need a technician to operate you.

Developing your body language starts with examining the nonverbal messages a speaker gives, including these:

- Proper speaking posture
- Gestures
- Body movement/walking patterns
- Facial expressions
- Eye contact
- Your overall appearance

When you present a speech, your listeners use their eyes and ears, as well as their own people instincts, to determine whether you

- are sincere.
- welcome the opportunity to speak to the audience.
- truly believe what you are saying.
- are interested in the audience and care about them.
- are confident and in control.

Here's another important credo:

Physical actions speak louder than words.

Consider the following example. Shuffling his notes, a man staggers to the podium. He clears his throat, grabs the lectern tightly, and plunges into his speech by saying, "It's a great pleasure to be here today. I have a message of extreme importance to you."

The effect of these opening remarks was anything but positive. Although his words expressed pleasure in addressing his audience, he transmitted a clearly contradictory nonverbal message: "I'm in terrible discomfort. I don't actually want to be anywhere near here."

This man's visual messages may have been generated by nervousness and inexperience or actual physical discomfort and were transmitted unconsciously. His nonverbal communication branded him as insincere, indifferent, and incompetent, even though he was none of these things.

When you speak, your audience tends to mirror your attitudes as they perceive them through their senses. For example, if you're unenthusiastic, your audience will feel that way, too. If you appear nervous, your audience will probably be nervous. If you fidget, they will perceive a lack of self-control in you and will be likely to doubt your message. It is vital, therefore, that your body faithfully portray your true feelings and intent, so that your body language doesn't work against your goals.

Providing a true barometer of your feelings and attitudes is the single greatest benefit of purposeful, effective physical action in public speaking. There are other benefits as well.

- Physical actions make messages more meaningful.
- People tend to become bored with things that don't move. They will naturally look at moving objects.
- Audiences remember messages that reach multiple senses. Therefore gestures, body movements, and facial expressions are valuable tools when employed skillfully.
- Physical actions punctuate your speeches. Written language includes an array of punctuation marks: commas, semicolons, periods, question marks,

exclamation points, and so on. However, when you speak, you use an entirely different set of symbols to show what part of your speech is most important and to add power and vitality to your words.

- Physical actions help relieve nervous tension. Being nervous before a speech is healthy. It shows that your speech is important to you. But using your body effectively can help dispel your nervousness once you start speaking.

Proper Speaking Posture

How you position your body when you speak communicates a set of visual messages to an audience. Good posture also helps you breathe properly and project your voice effectively. When you stand still, be careful not to sway or rock. Make sure both feet are planted firmly on the floor and your shoulders are square. Don't lean, slouch, or hunch over. When you walk, stand tall. Be proud of yourself—you have an important message to communicate!

Gestures

Gestures are specific body movements that reinforce a verbal message. Most gestures are made with your hands and arms. Your hands are marvelous tools of communication. A speaker's gestures can suggest very precise bits of meaning to an audience. To be effective, a speaker's gestures must be purposeful. They must also have the same meaning to the audience as they do to the speaker. Gestures reflect not only what is being said, but the personality behind the message.

- **Gestures clarify and support your words.** They strengthen the audience's understanding of your verbal message.
- **Gestures dramatize your ideas.** They help paint vivid pictures in your listeners' minds.
- **Gestures lend emphasis and vitality.** They underscore your feelings and attitudes.
- **Gestures help dissipate nervous tension.** They are a good outlet for nervous energy.
- **Gestures function as visual aids.** They enhance audience attentiveness and retention.
- **Gestures stimulate audience participation.** They help elicit the response you want.

Gestures are grouped into four categories:

1. **Descriptive gestures.** Are used to clarify or enhance. Some descriptive gestures include using your hands to indicate the size, shape, location, and function of something, like choppy ocean waves, a huge mountain, or a miniature creature.
2. **Emphatic gestures.** Underscore what is being said. For example, a clenched fist suggests strong feelings such as anger or determination.
3. **Suggestive gestures.** Are symbols of ideas or emotions. For example, an open palm suggests giving or receiving, while a shrug of the shoulders indicates ignorance, perplexity, or irony.
4. **Prompting gestures.** Are used to evoke a desired response from the audience. For example, if you want your listeners to raise their hands, applaud, or perform some other action, you will encourage the desired response by doing the act yourself as an example.

Location of Gestures

You can make gestures above, below, or at or near your shoulders; each position produces a different effect on your speech delivery.

1. Gestures above the shoulders suggest physical height, inspiration, or emotion.
2. Gestures below the shoulders indicate sadness, rejection, apathy, or condemnation.
3. Gestures at or near the shoulders suggest calmness, serenity.

The most frequently used gesture involves an open palm held outward toward the audience. As I said earlier, holding your palm outward implies giving or receiving. Unfortunately, most speakers use this gesture unconsciously as a general movement without any specific meaning. A palm held *downward* expresses suppression, secrecy, completion, or stability. A palm held *upward* and *outward* suggests stopping. Hands also imply measurement such as tall, short, small, long, and so on. As you practice your speech, experiment with different gestures to find those that both feel natural to you and underscore your message.

Don't Keep Your Hands to Yourself

There are speakers who, with a well-placed gesture, can move an audience to the edge of their seats. For many speakers, however, the only body movements included in their presentations are the frantic clutching of note cards and grasping the lectern for support. Body movement and gestures make or break a speech. You can motivate your audience through well-timed gestures, pacing, and, of course, eye contact.

Gestures should consist of purposeful movements of the

head, shoulders, arms, hands, and entire body. They should not be too repetitive.

All too often, when men stand up to speak, they immediately put their hands in their pockets. As they continue the presentation, their hands go deeper and deeper. When they eventually try to use their hands to gesture naturally, they find they're so deep in their pockets that they have difficulty getting them out. Men also have the habit of playing with their pocket change. This only draws your audience's attention to your hands and pockets and distracts them from listening to your message.

Women, on the other hand, have a habit of playing with their jewelry, hair, or clothes. For example, tugging at an earring, brushing their hair back with their fingers, or pulling their suit jacket down. Each of these habits is distracting to your audience.

International speaker David Peoples provides this list of distractions that are guaranteed to take the audience's attention off the subject.

- Rattling keys or coins in your pocket
- Using ums, uhs, and ya knows
- Sucking the teeth
- Twisting a ring
- Stroking a beard
- Lip licking
- Lip biting
- Tugging your ear
- Cracking your knuckles
- Pushing your glasses back on the bridge of your nose
- Playing with a watch

- Drumming your fingers
- Bouncing a pencil on its eraser
- Blowing hair out of your eyes
- Popping the top of a marker
- Extending and retracting a telescopic pointer
- Twirling hair
- Playing with beads, gold chains, or other jewelry

When a gesture is not necessary, make sure you have a natural resting place for your hands, such as by your side, or with the elbows slightly bent and hands at waist level, in preparation for your next gesture.

How to Gesture Effectively

Gestures are reflections of every speaker's individual personality. What's right for one speaker may not be right for another; however, if you apply the following seven rules, you can become a dynamic, confident speaker who uses gestures well.

1. **Respond naturally to what you think, feel, and see.** It's natural for you to gesture. If you inhibit your impulse to gesture, you'll probably become tense.
2. **Create the condition for gesturing, not the gesture.** When you speak, you should be totally involved in communicating—not thinking about your hands. Your gestures should be naturally motivated by the content of your presentation.
3. **Suit the action to the word and the occasion.** Your visual and verbal messages must function as partners in communicating the same thought or feeling. Every gesture you make should be purposeful and reflective of

your words so the audience will note only the effect, not the gesture itself.

4. **Don't overdo the gesturing.** You'll draw the listener away from your message. Young audiences are usually attracted to a speaker who uses vigorous gestures, but older, more conservative groups may feel your physical actions are overwhelming or irritating.
5. **Make your gestures convincing.** Your gestures need to be lively and distinct if they are to convey the intended impressions. Effective gestures are vigorous enough to be convincing yet slow enough and broad enough to be clearly visible without being overpowering. For example, if you are conveying excitement about a point or topic in your speech, show it in your face such as with a big smile. If you are excited and don't show it, your body language sends a negative message. Your gestures need to match your words and the mood you are conveying.
6. **Make your gestures smooth and well timed.** This rule is the most important but also the hardest. Why? Gestures have to be planned in advance so you can incorporate them during your speech rehearsal. In addition, practice sessions allow you to get a sense of how early you need to start your gesture so it coincides with the point you are making. Every gesture has three parts:
   - **The approach.** Your body begins to move in anticipation.
   - **The stroke.** The gesture itself.
   - **The return.** This brings your body back to a balanced posture.

The flow of a gesture—the approach, the stroke, the return—most be smoothly executed so that only the stroke is evident to the audience. While it's advisable to practice gesturing, don't try to memorize your every move. This makes your gesturing stilted and ineffective. For example, you're standing on the left-hand side of the stage (the audience's left) and you need to use the flip chart to illustrate a point, but the flip chart is on the far right-hand side of the stage (the audience's right). You may say to your audience, "Let's take a look at it on the flip chart."

As you start this statement begin walking toward the flip chart (the approach). Your goal is to start your gesture early enough so you can walk naturally toward the flip chart. At the word *flip chart* place your hand on the flip chart. This combined walking and placement of your hand on the flip chart is the gesture or the stroke. After a brief moment, place your hand on the flip chart and then take your hand and move it to one of your resting positions. This is the return or completion of the gesture.

7. **Make natural, spontaneous gesturing a habit.** The first step in becoming adept at gesturing is to determine what, if anything, you are doing now. For example, pay attention to the gestures you use in everyday conversations and try to use these gestures during your presentation. If you prefer, you can videotape your practice speech. For more on videotaping, see Day 8 and "Body Language" later in this chapter. The camcorder is truthful and unforgiving. If you want to become a more effective speaker, you need to make the camcorder your best friend. Recording yourself is a surefire way to eliminate your distracting mannerisms.

Videotape yourself and identify your bad habits. Then work at eliminating them.

To improve gestures, practice—but never during a speech. Practice gesturing when speaking informally to friends, family members, and co-workers.

Body Movement/Walking Patterns

Changing your position or location while speaking is the broadest, most visible physical action you can perform. Therefore it can either help drive your message home or spell failure for even the most well-planned speech.

Moving your body in a controlled, purposeful manner creates three benefits.

1. Supports and reinforces what you say
2. Attracts an audience's attention
3. Burns up nervous energy and relieves physical tension

However, body movement can work against you. Remember this one rule:

Never move without a reason.

As I said earlier, the eye is inevitably attracted to a moving object, so any body movement you make during a speech invites attention. Too much movement, even the right kind, can become distracting to an audience. Bear in mind the following types of body movement:

- Stepping forward during a speech suggests you are arriving at an important point.
- Stepping backward indicates you've concluded an idea and want the audience to relax for a moment.

- Lateral movement implies a transition; it indicates that you are leaving one thought and taking up another. For example, if you are standing in front of the audience and are ready to move on to your next point, move slowly sideways until you are standing next to the lectern.

The final reason for body movement is the easiest: *to get from one place to another.* In almost every speaking situation, you must walk from the location you are addressing your audience to your props, especially if you use visual aids. Always change positions by leading with the foot nearest your destination.

You may ask, Why move in the first place? Moving forces people to focus and follow you. The *way* you walk from your seat to the speaker's location is very important. When you are introduced, you should appear eager to speak. Many speakers look as though they are heading toward execution.

- Walk confidently from your seat to the lectern. Pause there a few seconds and then move out from behind the lectern. As discussed before, it is wise to use the lectern as a point of departure, not a barrier to hide behind.
- Smile before you say your first words.
- Don't stand too close or move beyond the first row of participants.
- Don't walk too much. It works against you. Continuous pacing is distracting.
- Walking stresses an important idea. It is essential that you walk with purpose and intention, not just a random shift of position. For example, taking about three steps, moving at a slight angle, usually works best.

- Use three positions with visual aids. Your "home" position is front and center. The other two positions should be relatively near the "home" position. You can move to the right of the podium and then to the left. Using and varying these three positions prevents you from favoring one side of the audience. If you're speaking on a stage, these three positions are called front center, stage left, and stage right. Never stand in front of any visual aid.
- Practice your walking patterns to and from your three positions. These positions should be planned just as your hand gestures are. For example, you want your body to move and gesture naturally. However, since most people are nervous about speaking in public, they tend to stiffen their muscles and hold back their natural tendency to gesture. Let your body tell you when it wants to move.
- Maintain good posture when you are not moving.

Tips You Must Know About Facial Expressions

Leave that deadpan expression to poker players. A good speaker realizes that appropriate facial expressions are an important part of effective communication. In fact, facial expressions are often the key determinant of the meaning behind the message. People watch a speaker's face during a presentation. When you speak, your face—more clearly than any other part of your body—communicates to your audience your attitudes, feelings, and emotions.

Dr. Paul Ekman of the University of California at San Francisco has made a career of studying facial expression and facial animation. He mapped out a technique for coding facial expressions called facial action coding system, FACS, based on the role facial muscles play in expressing different emotions. Ekman's research indicates that there are seven emotional expressions shared by everyone: sadness, happiness, anger, interest, fear, contempt, and surprise.

Here is a list of tips you need to know:

1. **Be yourself.** Don't try to copy the facial expression style of someone else. For example, just because your favorite professional speaker starts his or her presentations by telling a story using exaggerated facial expressions doesn't mean it will work for you.
2. **Don't overdo it.** Some people intentionally try to control their facial expressions by forcing themselves to smile or use another expression that isn't natural to them. Watch out for "fake" facial expressions that have a negative impact on your speech or compromise your sincerity.
3. **Practice in front of a mirror.** Notice what expressions you use while speaking. Study how to control your facial expressions. Ask yourself, Do they match my words?
4. **Create different moods.** While practicing in front of the mirror, see if your facial expressions convey the mood you want to create. If your face isn't showing any emotion, stop, refocus, and try again.
5. **Think about what you are saying.** Focus on your message and communicating with your audience, and your facial expressions follow.
6. **Smile before you begin.** As I've said before, the one true international nonverbal expression understood by all is the smile. A warm smile before you begin to speak

warms up an audience quickly, and ending with a smile puts your audience at ease with what they've just learned.

Eye Contact

One key element of facial expression is eye contact. It is estimated that 80 percent of nonverbal communication takes place with your face and your eyes. Eye contact is the cement that binds together speakers and their audiences. When you speak, your eyes involve your listeners in your presentation.

There is no faster way to break a communication bond between you and the audience than by failing to look at your listeners. No matter the size of your audience, *each listener* wants to feel that you are talking directly to him or her.

Looking at your listeners as individuals convinces them that you are sincere, are interested in them, and care whether or not they accept your message. Effective eye contact is also an important feedback device that makes the speaking situation a two-way communication process. By looking at your audience, you determine how they are reacting to your presentation.

How to Use Your Eyes Effectively

Your eyes convey a message to your audience. Here are tips to help you use your eyes to better communicate with your audience.

- **Know your material.** Know your material backward and forward, so you don't have to devote mental energy to scanning your note cards for the next topic (an audience interprets this latter behavior negatively, perceiving that you are unsure about what follows your last point). Prepare well and rehearse often so you don't have to depend heavily on notes.

- **Establish a visual bond.** Select one person and maintain eye contact with that person long enough to establish a visual bond, about five to ten seconds. Then shift your gaze to another person. In a small group, this is relatively easy. With larger crowds it's difficult. Instead select one or two individuals in each section of the room and establish personal bonds with them. This will leave each listener with the impression you're talking directly to him or her.
- **Monitor visual feedback.** While you are talking, your listeners are responding with their own nonverbal messages such as a smile or nod of the head. Use your eyes to seek out this valuable feedback. If individuals aren't looking at you, they may not be listening, either. Reasons for this include the following:

  —They can't hear you. Solution: If you are not using a microphone, speak louder.

  —They are bored. Solution: Use humor, increase your vocal variety, or add powerful gestures or body movements.

  —They are puzzled. Solution: Repeat or rephrase what you have just said.

  —They are fidgeting nervously. Solution: You may be using distracting mannerisms. Heighten your self-awareness of your voice and body language.

On the other hand, if your listeners' faces indicate interest and close attention, don't change a thing. You're doing a great job!

Your Overall Appearance

Wear your best suit or dress for your presentation, the outfit that elicits the most compliments. Make sure that every item of clothing is clean, pressed, and tailored. You know what type of attire to wear based on the information you learned from your preprogram and custom survey (Day 3) about your audience. Don't wear jewelry that might glitter or jingle when you move or gesture. This diverts attention from your speech. For the same reason, remove items and anything such as pocket change that makes noise when you move.

The first impression you give is completely related to your overall appearance and occurs even before you are introduced to deliver your speech. To convey a positive appearance as the audience arrives, you shouldn't be studying your speech, but rather mingling with the audience and projecting that same friendly, confident attitude you will use in your speech.

Body Language

Here are three ways to make your body speak effectively.

1. **Rid yourself of distracting mannerisms.** When your actions are intertwined with your words, the impact of your speech is strengthened. If your platform behavior includes mannerisms unrelated to your spoken message, those actions call attention to themselves and away from your speech. Eliminate vocal and visual impediments.

   You can easily correct a verbal mistake because you hear your own words. Since you can't see yourself, most distracting mannerisms go uncorrected. You can't eliminate them unless you know they exist. Again, the best way to correct this behavior is to videotape yourself.

Here is my four-step process for reviewing your videotape to free yourself of physical behaviors that distract from your speech:

- **Review #1.** Review your tape without looking for mannerisms. Just listen to the presentation and evaluate the *overall impact* you experience from watching the tape.
- **Review #2.** Turn the volume down and review your tape a second time. Look for *visual distractions* such as swaying your body, fixing your hair, or touching your face. Take notes on what you observe—note distracting mannerisms as well as gestures or other body movements that you feel work well.
- **Review #3.** Turn the picture off or turn away from the screen and listen only to *your voice.* The audience interprets and makes assumptions about your body language based on your verbal interpretations. Become accustomed to listening to your own voice. Get to know it as others hear it. Note what you like and dislike. Pay attention to the speed, volume, and the tone of your voice.
- **Review #4.** After you complete your list of distracting mannerisms and your more positive points, ask one or two family members to watch the tape with you. *Get their initial impression.* Ask them to be honest about the strengths and weaknesses of your mannerisms.

A great way to practice overcoming your distracting mannerisms is to pay attention to your mannerisms the next several times you have a conversation with a friend or family member.

2. **Let your body mirror your message.** If you are interested in your subject, believe what you are saying, and want to share your message with others, your physical movements come from within and are appropriate to what you are saying.

   For example, I was working with a company CEO who believed he shouldn't use his hands to communicate because he was Italian and felt he already "talked" too much with his hands. As a result of this belief, he intentionally restricted his movements and hand gestures. Subconsciously he created an image he felt he needed to protect and he put on a mask by not allowing his inner self to truly express what he was feeling. After working with him on this behavior and teaching him how to speak conversationally using hand gestures, I was able to fine-tune his gestures so they were more effective in communicating his message.

   To become an effective speaker, it is essential that you throw away your mask and share your true feelings with your audience. Your audience wants to know how *you* feel about your subject. If you want to convince others, you must convey *your* convictions. Remember this credo:

   Speak from the heart and to the soul.

3. **Use your everyday speaking situations to practice body language.** Whenever you speak to people, make an extra effort to notice *how* you speak. Observe your listener's facial expressions to see if he or she does or does not comprehend what you are saying. For example, a listener who is not making eye contact with you may not understand or may be bored. A listener who responds to your message, such as with a nod of

agreement, understands and is attentive to your presentation.

As an exercise to help you practice body language and gestures, prepare a ninety-second presentation about yourself. Describe who you are and what you do. Record your presentation and review it using the four-point process discussed in step one. Since you are talking about yourself, no research is required; however, you do need to prepare what you are going to say and how you are going to say it. Plan everything, including your gestures and walking patterns.

Confidence Builder: Voice Tips Guaranteed to Entrance Your Audience

No matter what you believe, there is no such thing as the "perfect voice." Each individual voice is as unique as the person's hairstyle and manner of dress. Nothing is worse than listening to a speaker with a monotone voice. While your visual presentation has a big impact on your audience, your tone of voice is also very important. How you sound and the manner in which you vary your voice has a notable effect on your listeners.

Top Ten List: Tips for Creating a Confident Voice

- **Have a conversation with your audience.** Think about your message, and just think of your speech as having a conversation with your audience. For example, think of your audience as a friend you talk to often.

- **Talk loudly enough.** Make sure that your audience can hear you. Use a microphone if necessary. If the audience cannot hear you, they will tune you out.
- **Use expression in your voice.** If you truly believe in what you are saying, this will communicate through the expression in your voice.
- **Pronounce your words carefully.** Take the time to learn proper pronunciation. Nothing is worse than watching a speaker stumble over words.
- **Do not speak too fast.** This is one of the most common problems speakers have. Many people speak too fast because of nervousness. Watch your speed!
- **Do not use filler words such as "um," "ah," or "okay."** Spend time and learn to eliminate these filler words.
- **Increase your volume to convey excitement.** Show excitement in your voice, but be careful not to yell.
- **Decrease your volume to evoke emotion.** Lowering your volume is an effective way to show your emotions. Just be careful not to speak too softly.
- **Change your speed to match your audience's needs.** I speak to a variety of age groups ranging from older adults to elementary students. In general, with older groups I speak more slowly. Since I usually speak on the faster side, this is a challenge for me. A younger audience, on the other hand, looks for fast-paced presentations and a speaker who demonstrates high energy.

  I also use speed to "wake up" an audience. If a previous speaker has effectively put the audience to sleep, I use speed to reenergize them. I use this speed in connection with animated movement, but I make sure I still speak clearly so the audience understands my message.

- **Use proper breathing.** Inhale and exhale fully to assure that you project your voice clearly and provide the necessary air support to your voice.

Tip of the Day

There are times when you may be asked to step in for a co-worker and give a presentation with only a few moments to prepare. Take into consideration that you were most likely asked to speak because you have knowledge about the topic. The most important thing—don't panic. If you can, find a copy of the presentation handouts and scan them, writing down the main topics for each portion of the presentation. This allows you to quickly look at the content of the presentation. If the original speaker planned to use slides, quickly skim each slide and write down the key points. Do not concern yourself with using the exact words on the slide. If the slides are properly prepared, each will have only a few key phrases—your talking points for each section of the presentation.

In the event you don't have a co-worker's handouts or slides, quickly develop an outline or mind map (see Day 8) and do the following:

- List your main points and write down a few key words about each.
- Speak spontaneously and confidently from your heart.
- Trust your experience and knowledge.
- Focus on your message and not on the fact that you had to rush to put together a presentation.

In Day 6 I will discuss the use of language and ethics in your speech, along with tips on how to use humor. In addition, I will discuss ten famous speeches from history and what you can learn from them.

Day 6

Language and Ethics

Today I will focus on the language of giving speeches. Speech language includes elements such as the following:

- alliteration
- clichés
- metaphors and similes
- imagery

How you incorporate the various language components depends on your own speaking style and comfort level.

As a professional speaker, I write speeches for business professionals, but I have also been hired to write speeches for brides, bridegrooms, best men, teachers, administrators, politicians, and even ministers. Although the written style for each is unique, all my clients ask that their speeches come across as conversational. Being able to write conversationally can be a challenge, but with a strong working knowledge of the range of language elements at your disposal, it does get easier.

The Elements of Language

Let's look at the various elements of language and some tips to help you use them in each of your speeches. However, avoid overuse of these elements because they can become distractions for your audience and may steer them away from listening to your message.

Alliteration

An alliteration is a sentence or long phrase in which each of the words begins with the same letter. Two common alliterations most of you are familiar with are "She sells seashells by the seashore" and "Peter Piper picked a peck of pickled peppers." Alliteration can be used to make a point memorable in your presentation or to convey dramatic or poetic nuances. This technique also gives the listener a catchy phrase to remember a particular message. The following examples use this repeated letter technique. Think about how you can use alliteration in your speeches and presentations. Have fun with it.

In my workshops I use an alliteration I call the nine *P*'s: Prior Proper Preparations Prevents Poor Performance of the Person Putting on the Presentation. Another alliteration I use represents the three *R*'s of motivation:

- Recognition
- Reward
- Reinforcement

Clichés

Clichés are short, trite phrases that refer to commonly held ideas but have lost their originality owing to overuse. "Look on the bright side" is one example of a cliché. Here are several others:

- Live and learn.
- What goes around comes around.
- Don't worry, be happy.
- Today is the first day of the rest of your life.
- No pain, no gain.
- Every cloud has a silver lining.
- Every rose has its thorn.
- Cheer up, it's not the end of the world.
- It could be worse.

You get the idea. Using clichés in your speeches is very effective as long as they fit with your message. For example, if you are giving a motivational speech to a group of people starting a new exercise program, the cliché "No pain, no gain" may very well be appropriate to use. One cliché I use when working with clients who are uncomfortable speaking in front of people is "Cheer up, it's not the end of the world." I explain to the client that he must conquer his fear of public speaking and believe that the audience will like him and be interested in his message.

Metaphors and Similes

A metaphor is a figurative comparison between two usually unconnected things, resulting in an image in the mind's eye. For example, the statement "My love is a rose" is a metaphor. The message the listener gets is that, like a rose, love is fragile and beautiful yet thorny.

Like a metaphor, a simile is a figure of speech where two usually unconnected things are compared, often in a phrase introduced by "like" or "as." For example, "My love is like a red, red rose."

It is common to use metaphors or similes to express feelings, ideas, and concepts that are complex or hold a special meaning for you, or to paint a particular, even humorous, image for the audience. In a motivational speech to get a participant to feel good about him- or herself, I used the simile "You look like a million bucks."

Exercise: Metaphor or Simile

Come up with a metaphor or simile to describe how you might feel in the following situations.

1. Getting an A on a final exam when you would have been happy to have gotten a C.
2. Your first experience of speaking anxiety or stage fright.
3. Witnessing a serious accident.

Imagery

Imagery is the use of vivid or figurative language to represent objects, actions, or ideas. In seminars I use imagery to tell a story. Imagery is a wonderful technique to help you convey your message and help individuals "picture" abstract concepts. Also, I use imagery to help clients have more self-confidence and self-esteem when they are preparing to speak in front of a group of people. When I use imagery in my presentations I use three objects related to my topic and describe each. For example, let's say your topic is job hunting and you decide to use imagery to discuss the job interview process and three types of job candidates. Here are three images you might choose to use to describe these candidates:

- **Overkill.** The individual who arrives at the job interview wearing an extremely expensive suit, with his hair slicked back, and carrying an attaché case, laptop, and cell phone.
- **Professional.** The individual who arrives at the interview ten minutes early wearing a clean, well-pressed, fashionable but conservative suit, with her hair neatly swept off her face, and carrying a slim portfolio and small purse.
- **Laid back.** The individual who strolls into the interview fifteen minutes late wearing wrinkled pants and an untucked, collarless shirt, with his hair unkempt, scraggly facial hair, and holding a dog-eared resume in his hand.

Danger Zone: Ethics

In preparing any speech it is crucial to develop and use your own material. It is unethical to use someone else's stories, data, or research and try to pass it off as your own. Using unattributed material is called plagiarism and is illegal. If you develop and use *your own* material, you won't find yourself on the wrong end of a lawsuit.

If you do, however, find information or data from another source that supports your claim or ideas, you can get the author's permission in writing *before* you use the information, or if it's from a research study or professional journal you can attribute the information in a verbal citation in your speech. For example, "According to data by the Gallup Organization . . ." It is unethical to use other people's material (even something by a colleague) without

- asking them.
- giving proper credit in the speech.

I continually receive calls from businesses, colleges, and authors asking for permission to reprint one of my articles. In return I expect proper credit. In my career as a public speaker, I have experienced only a few incidences when an individual has actually taken my articles word for word and tried to pass them off as his or her own. This is not only unethical, but also in violation of copyright laws.

Positive Performance: What You Need to Know About Plagiarism

Northwestern University's "Principles Regarding Academic Integrity" defines plagiarism to its students as "submitting material that in part or whole is not entirely [the writer's or speaker's] own work without attributing those same portions to their correct source." Plagiarism occurs in many forms other than writing, such as art, music, computer code, mathematics, and scientific work.

To help you, here are Northwestern University's guidelines for proper attribution.

Guidelines for Proper Attribution

As you plan a speech, you will likely draw from a vast pool of texts, ideas, and findings that individuals have accumulated over hundreds, even thousands, of years. What you call originality is actually the innovative combining, amending, or extending of material from that pool.

The most helpful form of attribution is a citation where you give precise information about your source: where the material came from, the author's name, and the publication date. At times it is difficult to know what needs to be cited.

Common knowledge or ideas that have been in the public domain and are found in a number of sources don't need to be cited. One example of a document that doesn't require a citation is the Bill of Rights. If you are in doubt, document.

As someone who is learning to develop your own speaking style, you may want to emulate your favorite professional speaker and copy certain styles and techniques. Professional speakers, myself included, are very sensitive to having individuals use our personal stories in their seminar or keynote address. Develop your own stories that can relate to your message.

- Learn when to give proper attribution. An attribution is necessary in a speech when something you say might leave listeners in doubt about whom you are attributing the material to and for what reason.
- Respect the source. Make sure your attribution expresses your appreciation for being allowed to borrow the information. For example, at the end of your speech you could say to the audience, "I would like to take this opportunity to thank Herb Johnson for his compelling work in the area of foster care in inner cities."

Top Ten List: Influential and Memorable Speeches in History

Following are what I believe to be the ten most influential and memorable speeches in history. Notice that I have not included entire speeches, just excerpts.

1. **The Gettysburg Address.** By Abraham Lincoln on November 19, 1863. "Four score and seven years ago, our fathers brought forth on this continent, a new

nation, conceived in Liberty, and dedicated to the proposition that all men are created equal." I am sure you have read this address—one of the best-known speeches of American history—given by our sixteenth president during the Civil War. This speech is amazingly powerful even though it was only about two minutes long. Over time, the Gettysburg Address and its closing message—"government of the people, by the people, for the people"—have come to symbolize the definition of democracy itself.

2. **Liberty or death.** By Patrick Henry on March 23, 1775. Following the Boston Tea Party on December 16, 1773, in which American colonists dumped 342 chests of tea into Boston Harbor, the British Parliament enacted a series of so-called Intolerable Acts in response to the rebellion in Massachusetts. Henry's impassioned words "Forbid it, Almighty God! I know not what course others may take; but as for me, give me liberty or give me death!" influenced Virginia's government to support his resolutions, which in turn propelled Virginia into the American Revolution.
3. **On women's right to vote.** By Susan B. Anthony in 1873. In the 1880s women in the United States were legal underdogs who did not even have the right to vote. Susan B. Anthony gave a speech after she was arrested for casting an illegal vote in the presidential election of 1872. She was fined $100 but refused to pay. In her speech she stated, "Webster, Worcester, and Bouvier all define a citizen to be a person in the United States, entitled to vote and hold office. The only question left to be settled now is: Are women persons? And I hardly believe any of our opponents will have the hardihood to say they are not. Being persons, then, women are

citizens; and no state has a right to make any law, or to enforce any old law, that shall abridge their privileges or immunities. Hence, every discrimination against women in the constitution and laws of the several states is today null and void."

Following her death in 1906 after decades of tireless work, both the Democratic and Republican parties endorsed women's right to vote.

4. **"I have a dream."** By Martin Luther King, August 28, 1963. King gave the keynote speech at the 1963 March on Washington for Jobs and Freedom, from the steps of the Lincoln Memorial, in front of about 250,000 people. Since 1963, King's "I have a dream" speech has become the most famous public address of the twentieth century. With his profound and far-reaching words, King cemented his place as a crusader for civil rights leadership.

   Here is the closing of his speech:

   "Let freedom ring. And when this happens, and when we allow freedom to ring—when we let it ring from every village and every hamlet, from every state and every city, we will be able to speed up that day when all of God's children—black men and white men, Jews and Gentiles, Protestants and Catholics—will be able to join hands and sing in the words of the old Negro spiritual: Free at last! Free at last! Thank God Almighty, we are free at last!"

5. **For a declaration of war.** By Franklin D. Roosevelt on December 8, 1941. On Sunday, December 7, 1941, the first assault wave of Japanese fighter planes attacked the U.S. naval base at Pearl Harbor, Hawaii, taking the Americans completely by surprise. On Monday, December 8, President Roosevelt appeared before

Congress and made his speech asking for a declaration of war against Japan, calling the previous day "a date which will live in infamy": "I ask that Congress declare that since the unprovoked and dastardly attack by Japan on Sunday, December 7, 1941, a state of war has existed between the United States and the Japanese empire."

6. **"We choose to go to the moon."** By John F. Kennedy on September 12, 1962. In this 1962 speech made at Rice University in Houston, Texas, President John F. Kennedy reaffirmed America's commitment to landing a man on the moon before the end of the 1960s. The president spoke in philosophical terms about the need to solve the mysteries of space and also defended the enormous expense of the program. "Well, space is there, and we're going to climb it, and the moon and the planets are there, and new hopes for knowledge and peace are there. And, therefore, as we set sail we ask God's blessing on the most hazardous and dangerous and greatest adventure in which man has ever embarked."
7. **"I am prepared to die."** By Nelson Mandela on April 20, 1964. In 1962 Nelson Mandela was arrested by South African security police for his opposition to the white government and its apartheid ("separateness") policies of racial, political, and economic discrimination against the nonwhite majority. In 1964 the government brought further charges against Mandela, including sabotage, high treason, and conspiracy to overthrow the government. This was part of Mandela's statement at the opening of his defense trial in April 1964: "During my lifetime I have dedicated myself to this struggle of the African people. I have fought against white domination, and I have fought against black

domination. I have cherished the ideal of a democratic and free society in which all persons live together in harmony and with equal opportunities. It is an ideal which I hope to live for and to achieve. But if needs be, it is an ideal for which I am prepared to die."

8. **"We shall overcome."** By Lyndon B. Johnson on March 15, 1965. In this eloquent speech to Congress, President Lyndon B. Johnson used the phrase *we shall overcome,* borrowed from African American leaders struggling for equal rights. The speech came a week after deadly racial violence erupted in Selma, Alabama, as African Americans were attacked by police while preparing to march to Montgomery to protest voting rights discrimination. "What happened in Selma is part of a far larger movement which reaches into every section and state of America. It is the effort of American Negroes to secure for themselves the full blessings of American life. Their cause must be our cause too. Because it is not just Negroes, but really it is all of us, who must overcome the crippling legacy of bigotry and injustice. And we shall overcome."
9. **Resigning the presidency.** By Richard M. Nixon on August 8, 1974. A unique and tragic event in American politics occurred as President Richard M. Nixon spoke on TV in August of 1974 to the American public, announcing his decision to resign the presidency. Nixon's decision came after the Judiciary Committee of the House of Representatives voted to recommend his impeachment. During the Senate investigation, a Nixon aide revealed the president had installed a bugging system in the Oval Office that had recorded most conversations on tape. Under intense pressure in the spring of 1974, Nixon released edited transcripts of the

tapes containing his conversations. "I have never been a quitter. To leave office before my term is completed is abhorrent to every instinct in my body. But as president, I must put the interest of America first. America needs a full-time president and a full-time Congress, particularly at this time with problems we face at home and abroad. . . . Therefore, I shall resign the presidency effective at noon tomorrow. . . ."

10. **Recognition of the American Basketball League and the Women's National Basketball Association.** By Congresswoman Corrine Brown on June 17, 1997. Congresswoman Corrine Brown gave this speech before Congress, asking them to sign a bill acknowledging the establishment of two new women's professional basketball leagues: the American Basketball League (ABL) and the Women's National Basketball Association (WNBA). "The success of women's sports has proved that America is ready for women's professional basketball. We have built a generation of talented players who can compete internationally, and now it is time to showcase this talent here in our own country. These leagues will offer role models to younger women and promote greater chances for female athletes, continuing the tradition of gender equity in sports. . . ."

Confidence Builder: Humor Goes a Long Way

Here are what I believe to be the top ten ways to be funny, taken from *Wake 'Em Up!—How to Use Humor and Other Pro-*

fessional Techniques to Create Alarmingly Good Business Presentations, by my colleague Tom Antion.

1. **Anachronisms.** An anachronism is a person, place, or thing that is out of its proper or chronological order. For instance, Paul Revere riding a motorcycle or George Washington sitting in front of a computer are humorous anachronisms. Any time you include an anachronistic relationship, you evoke humor and create more attention to your example, message, or point. Here's a good fill-in-the-blank format. Would [big name from the past] have ______ if he had ______? All you have to do is make a simple relationship, and your message will be funny and memorable. For example: Would George Washington have thrown his money away in the Potomac if he had Fidelity Investment Management Associates on his side?
2. **Audience gags.** Audience gags are offbeat jokes that occur unexpectedly during a presentation. Dr. Joel Goodman developed this gag: A telephone rings during his presentation. He answers a phone that is hidden in the lectern and pretends to talk to his mother. The same joke would be called a "running gag" if the phone rang at several other times during the program.

   One of the more effective gags or skits I use in my program is the telephone exercise. In this exercise I choose two participants and have them sit in chairs with their backs to one another. I have one person pretend to call the other person with the objective of asking permission to send information. What the individual doesn't know is that the person receiving the call has been instructed to *not* agree to anything without his or her boss's permission. The person placing the call must use all possible sales and presentation techniques to convince the other person without getting angry. While this conversation is going on, I have the rest of the audience record the nonverbal expressions on each person's face. When the conversation is concluded, the audience discusses the volunteer's body language. The purpose of this exercise is to demonstrate that we use body language when we are on the phone even though the person we are speaking to cannot see us. The exercise also shows the audience how to remain professional, keep their cool, and gain a better understanding of how we use body language.

3. **What is he talking about?** One of Tom's favorite gags is the false guest speaker. During this impersonation, Tom begins his presentation passing himself off as someone else. You can be as creative as you want with your impostor. He begins his speech pretending to know what he is talking about so it comes across as believable and authentic. He reveals his true identity only after he moves forward with his speech and starts to confuse the audience by talking about unrelated topics. Use this routine when you want to reduce audience pressure or just want to have some fun before you begin your speech. You can vary the length of the impostor's speech to suit your program.
4. **Cartoons.** One of the most universally accepted forms of humor are cartoons. Here are three ways to use cartoons in your speeches:
    - Tell the audience about a cartoon you saw.
    - Cut out the cartoon from its publication and show it to your audience. Make sure you get permission before using it in your program.

- Make up a cartoon yourself. For example, when I give my speech "Overcoming Speaking Anxiety," I use a cartoon depicting a speaker backed into a corner with a terrified look on his face. This cartoon represents how my clients sometimes feel trapped in a corner when they have to speak in front of a group.

5. **Comic verse.** Often a short poem illustrates your point better than hours of meaningless talking. Poems can be inspiring and motivating as well as funny. They also add variety to your presentations. You must flawlessly memorize any comic verse you use. Any stumble ruins the effect of the verse. If the verse is long, you may want to read it, but complete memorization has more impact. I don't usually use comic verse in my presentations; however, when I do use a comic verse, it's at the end of my presentation to leave the audience with something to remember.

   Sid Madwed, a very good friend and colleague of mine, is a professional poet and uses comic verse in many of his speeches. Here is an example of comic verse that Sid wrote about public speaking.

   I know someone who can talk a blue streak.
   Yet, if asked to speak in public says he'll freak.
   Is it any wonder that speaking in public is man's great fear?
   Ask a hundred to speak in public and none will volunteer.
   For most would feel funny and some will feel queer.
   But great power is yours if in public you speak with ease.
   For you can share what you know in a way that will please.
   For those who master speaking in public have the power of a Hercules.
   (Used with permission from Sid Madwed, www.madwed.com.)

6. **Exaggeration.** Expanding or diminishing proportions of your speech can be a fun way to create humor. It's similar to a caricature artist who outrageously exaggerates the features of an individual while still keeping the person recognizable. For example, Tom gave a talk for Secretary's Day at a large insurance company and focused on how hectic it always was for the secretaries. This is how he incorporated exaggeration into his presentation: "You're answering the telephone, the fax machine is ringing, you're making copies, and you're filing every policy clear back to 1910." The secretaries could relate to each item mentioned. They did a lot of filing, but certainly not as far back as 1910. Exaggerating this date lent humor while driving home the point that they always had lots of work piled up.
7. **Fake facts and statistics.** Stating falsehoods as if they were absolutely true is another fun way to play with the audience. However, you must make the statements obviously false by your words and your facial expressions. You don't want to leave any doubt about whether you are joking or being serious.

   For example, here is how Tom incorporated fake statistics into his presentation: "A study done for the Alaskan Pipeline Workers Union indicated that 97.2 percent of Alaskan Pipeline Workers wear panty hose." When giving fake statistics, use exact numbers for emphasis.
8. **Roast humor.** Being roasted (a tribute in which the honoree's friends and acquaintances alternate short speeches of praise and jokes) is a lot of fun, but you must be careful to honor the person you are roasting. Make jokes about things that are obviously untrue and

then exaggerate to make the humor even more obvious. Or you can outrageously exaggerate things about the individual that are true. Here is an example: "The emcee's job is not to be wise or witty. In fact, it is his job to appear dull so that the other speakers will shine in comparison. Considering who we are roasting tonight, it looks like I'm going to have to rise to new heights of boredom."

9. **Quotations.** Quotations are a safe bet to use: If they are not funny, you don't have to worry because you didn't write them. However, quotations can still be used to make your point. Thousands of notable quotations are available from quotation dictionaries, literature, and professional journals. Here are a few examples:

   "Get your facts first and then you can distort them as much as you please," by Mark Twain.

   "When you get to the end of your rope, tie a knot and hang on," by Franklin Delano Roosevelt.

10. **Self-effacing humor.** Self-effacing humor, or making fun of yourself, gets its strength from highlighting your own weaknesses. People who have the ability to laugh at themselves are perceived as secure, confident, strong, and likable. With this type of humor, a little goes a long way. If you overdo it, you will look like a doomsayer who is always putting yourself down. Seek out opportunities to tease yourself or make fun of your mistakes. This will be one of your most powerful tools to connect with the audience and a subtle way to show your strength.

   In my seminars I talk about the bad speaking habits I used to have and demonstrate a few by overexaggerating the gestures so that they look funny, but toned down enough so they're realistic. For example, I used to rise up and down on the balls of my feet. As I'm telling the audience about this behavior, I repeatedly rise up and down on the balls of my feet while swaying from side to side. The audience usually ends up laughing, and this tells them I'm not afraid to poke fun at myself.

Type of Speech: Informative

In Day 3 I discussed the different types of speeches: informative, demonstrative, persuasive, ceremonial, and impromptu or extemporaneous. Starting in this chapter and continuing through the remaining chapters of this book, I will give a portion of a sample speech so you can get a flavor of the different types of speeches and how to approach them. In this chapter I will share a portion of an informative speech. An informative speech gives the audience specific information about a certain topic or event.

When I was still working as a nuclear materials engineer, I gave this speech—"Nuclear Power and How it Works"—to high school science classes studying nuclear power.

Nuclear power is one of those things that keeps us in the light but so many of us are in the dark about it. Today, I am here to shed a little light on the subject and talk to you about nuclear power and how it works.

To begin, let's take a look at how steam is created. Imagine a flask of water being heated by a flame and eventually you see the water begin to boil. After the water boils, it begins to generate steam, causing a whistling sound to come from the flask. The same result happens when you heat the flask with a hot plate. The only difference was the heat source, flame vs. hot plate.

A nuclear power plant heats water the exact same way except the heat source is uranium dioxide, a special form of ura-

nium. When the uranium splits apart, it gives off heat and in turn heats the water to a boil.

You may be asking why I selected a speech from my former career. As a professional speaker you are asked to make presentations on complicated, technical material. This speech worked well because I used simple terms and tried to explain the nuclear fission process using analogies and real-world examples that the students could relate to.

Tip of the Day

When you really get serious about improving your presentation and speaking skills, you will probably want professional coaching. A good speaking coach can objectively evaluate where you are now in your speaking abilities and help you formulate a plan to reach your goals. There are no quick fixes, but you can make significant improvement quickly, maybe in only a few weeks, if you work at it and have the proper direction.

A speaking coach can evaluate you in person or with the help of a video or an audiotape. This tape is reviewed and an assessment is completed analyzing your strong points and what areas need improvement. If you are looking for a speaking coach, you can find a listing in the Yellow Pages or on the Internet. When you are talking with speaking coaches, whether on the phone or in person, be candid. Ask the coach for a list of clients he or she has worked with and testimonials from these clients. Ask how many years of experience the coach has in the field, if he or she has published any books, videos, or audiotapes. After gathering all the information, take time to review the facts and select a coach who will work best for you.

* * *

In Day 7 I will discuss how you deal with the unexpected—things that could and will go wrong. I will share some professional stories of the unexpected occurrences that have happened to me in my speaking career.

Day 7

Expect the Unexpected

There comes a time when you have put your heart and soul into preparing your presentation. You have spent hours, if not days, making sure you have reviewed all your notes, visual aids, and gestures and verified that the room in which you will be giving your presentation is reserved. However, when you arrive at the location, you find that something is wrong with the room, the equipment, or both.

Preparing for the unexpected, such as your slides falling in a puddle or drawing a complete blank just as you step up to the lectern, is the focus of this chapter. I will provide you with tips and ad libs to use when you find yourself in deep trouble. Furthermore, I will share secrets that professional speakers, trainers, and entertainers use to get themselves out of a jam.

These ideas and suggestions will work only if you plan for them beforehand and practice how to handle them. The more you anticipate problems ahead of time, the better prepared you are if they should happen. And believe me, there will come a time when *something* will creep up on you before or during your presentation.

Worrying about these situations leads to speaking anxiety, nervousness, and a lack of self-confidence; however, if you accept the fact that problems happen, you can better prepare yourself for the unexpected.

How to Prepare for the Unexpected

Novice public speakers believe that their presentation needs to be perfect or the audience will not respect them. This belief couldn't be further from the truth. Audiences, by nature, *want* you to succeed and are willing to help make it happen.

Let's look at some classic problems that many speakers (including myself) have experienced, such as problems with microphones, PA systems, overhead projectors, slide projectors, or the dais itself. In addition, I will discuss real-life situations that have occurred for many professional speakers and offer solutions to prevent, or at least minimize, these problems.

Microphone Problems

Today speakers use several different types of microphones, and each takes practice to learn how to use properly. For instance, holding a microphone in your hand while speaking is different from speaking into a microphone attached to the lectern.

- **Problem number 1.** The microphone goes dead in the middle of your presentation.

  Solution. In the event your microphone goes dead in the middle of your presentation, and you don't have a spare, turn off the microphone. Apologize to the audience. Then walk out to where the audience is sitting so they can hear you and make sure you project your voice to the back of the room. When you reach a breaking point in your speech, stop and see if you can locate another microphone.

- **Problem number 2.** Distortion problems. This includes problems such as popping noises—sounds caused by your mouth when you say words that begin with the letter *p*.

  Solution. Move your mouth farther away from the microphone and turn your head away slightly. If you are using a wireless microphone, adjust it by moving it to another location near you.

Visual Aid/Media Problems

The more audiovisual equipment you use in your presentation, the more likely it is that something will go wrong. It is very important that you take the time to set up your equipment properly and make sure it is working.

- **Problem number 1.** You accidentally drop your note cards and they get out of order.

  Solution. Make sure your note cards are numbered. In the event you drop them, you can quickly place them in their correct order. Try to do this without bringing attention to the notes. Also, do not have too many notes, so you don't have too many cards to shuffle.

- **Problem number 2.** Your equipment stops working altogether.

  Solution. If you cannot quickly determine and correct the problem, continue your presentation without the visual aids. Don't make your audience wait while you fix the problem. If you absolutely need the visual aids, take a short break to correct the malfunction.

- **Problem number 3.** Your slide carousel jams.

  Solution. Turn off the slide projector before you attempt to unjam the slide. Usually a slide gets stuck if it's not properly in line with the slide carousel. Use a pair of tweezers to remove the slide.

- **Problem number 4.** The overhead projector bulb burns out. This is probably the most common overhead projector problem.

  Solution. Always have a spare bulb. Some of the better overhead projectors have a spare bulb built into the projector, and all you have to do is slide the bulb selection lever over for the new bulb. This works if (and only if) the spare bulb works and did not burn out when the last person used it. This has happened many times! Make sure you have a spare bulb, the correct spare bulb, and know how to change the bulb.

  Note: Keep in mind that the bulb currently in the projector may still be hot and you will burn yourself if you touch it.

  Unplug the projector and, using a towel or cloth, remove the old bulb and replace it with a new one. Since this can take a few minutes, I would suggest you call a break to give yourself time to do this without the entire room watching you fumble with the projector. Spend time during your initial setup learning how to change the bulb. You will be glad you did. Each projector is unique, and the procedure to change the bulb is different with each. If you do end up using the spare bulb, remember to have the hotel replace it so the next person does not get a surprise.

Room Lighting

Many times it will be necessary to raise or lower the lighting in the room you are speaking in. Knowing where the lighting controls are and how to adjust the lighting is critical.

- **Problem number 1.** The sconces (lighting fixtures on the wall) don't appear to have any switches to control them, and they cast a bright light.
  Solution. I have run across this problem a lot and usually end up having to loosen the light bulbs to turn them off. It may be that only one or two lights are causing the problem, but check out this detail during your setup.

Platform Problems

Sometimes it is necessary to speak from a raised platform or stage. Since most platforms are temporary and set up just for an event, it is important for your own safety to make sure the platform is properly supported.

- **Problem number 1.** The platform is unstable.
  Solution. Walk the entire platform to check its sturdiness. Also, see how noisy the platform is when you walk across it. Check to make sure there are sturdy steps to walk up to the raised platform and that they are properly supported.

Confidence Builder: Great Icebreakers

Seldom is an icebreaker used when a keynote speech is given; however, most of you have probably attended a training session or seminar where you participated in an icebreaker game before the program started. Most of these icebreakers are intended to encourage participants to interact with one another. This is especially important if it's an all-day or multiday program.

An icebreaker is used to stress a particular point or just to have fun. Here are some of my favorite icebreakers.

Getting Acquainted

Objective: To have first-time participants attending a training session get acquainted with one another and to help build a climate of friendliness among guests.

Materials required: Blank stick-on tags.

Approximate time required: Flexible, depending on the group size. Maximum time is fifteen minutes.

Procedure: Give each person a blank name tag and ask each guest to write his or her first name or nickname on it. Have each guest list five words or brief phrases that describe something about him or her and can be used as conversation starters (residence, hobbies, children, and so on). Let's take a look at how my name tag would read.

Name: Lenny

1. Connecticut resident
2. Professional speaker
3. Semiprofessional musician
4. Married 25 years
5. Two children

After giving the group about five minutes to complete the task, have them separate into clusters of two and three. Every few minutes tell the group to "change partners" in order to encourage everyone to meet as many people as possible.

Discussion Questions

Here's a list of questions to ask attendees once they have gotten to know one another.

1. Was this exercise helpful to you in getting to know some other people in the training session?
2. What kind of information had the greatest impact on you?
3. How do you now feel about your involvement in this group?

Getting Acquainted Again

It's okay to have your workshop participants meet one another more than once.

Objective: To allow participants to become better acquainted through a structured exercise.

Material required: Blank name tags.

Approximate time required: Between fifteen and twenty minutes depending on the size of the group.

Procedure: At the opening session of a group meeting, give each individual a blank name tag. Have each person complete the following items with five- or 10-word responses.

1. My name is ______.
2. I have a question about ______.
3. I can answer questions about ______.

After a few minutes encourage attendees to seek out other attendees who can answer or be asked a question. Let the group mingle for ten to fifteen minutes.

Camouflage for a Departure

Here is an icebreaker to use at a large conference when you did not have the opportunity to do an audience questionnaire beforehand. It will allow attendees to bow out gracefully, if they realize they are in the wrong room.

Objective: To ensure at a large conference that attendees select the right session and to allow an opportunity to quickly become acquainted with the attendees.

Materials required: None.

Approximate time required: Five minutes.

Procedure: At large conferences the program description for individual sessions does not always accurately describe what the speaker or content will cover. Once the session starts, the attendees may discover the session is not what they originally thought but are reluctant to leave. This icebreaker takes care of that situation.

At the start of the session, paraphrase the session description in the program book, include objectives, and briefly indicate precisely what the session covers. Say to your attendees, "There may be some people in the room who now realize this session may not cover what they thought it would. Since it may be awkward or uncomfortable to get up and leave, let's all stand now, meet a few new people, and those of you who want to excuse yourselves can do so easily." Then have the group make three or four new acquaintances for two to three minutes.

There are hundreds, if not thousands, of icebreakers and games you can include in your seminars. The best source for ideas is a series of books by Edward E. Scannell:

- *Games Trainers Play* (McGraw-Hill, Inc., 1989)
- *Still More Games Trainers Play* (McGraw-Hill, Inc., 1991)
- *More Games Trainers Play* (McGraw-Hill, Inc., 1993)
- *Even Still More Games Trainers Play* (McGraw-Hill, Inc., 1994)

Tips from the Experts: How to Recognize and Take Advantage of a Spontaneous Moment

Spontaneity is fundamental to the success of your presentation and plays an important role in your credibility. You lose a chance to connect with your audience by not taking advantage of a spontaneous opportunity. Tony Jeary, author of *Inspire Any Audience,* says a joke by an audience member, a piece of timely news, even a mistake you make, are all spontaneous moments you can use to win the respect of your audience and strengthen your credibility.

The irony in spontaneity is that to be spontaneous, you have to be prepared. Mark Twain once said, "It takes about six weeks to prepare a good ad-lib comment." The truth is that you can plan spontaneity. Leave space for responding to the unexpected in your presentation. For example, don't be afraid to detour from your presentation to go in a promising direction opened up by a question from the audience.

One example where I took advantage of a spontaneous

moment was a speaking engagement in Poughkeepsie, New York, near the airport. I was talking about external noises and how they can be distracting. Just as I was discussing the various types of distractions, a jumbo jet flew over the hotel, making its usual loud noise. It got so loud, in fact, that I had to stop speaking. After the jet passed, I turned to the audience and said, "Do you know how much I paid that pilot to do that? I love it when people follow their cues on time." The audience was hysterical, and that moment really drove my point home.

Outtakes: The Biggest Flub-ups and How the Speakers Covered Themselves

In previous chapters I discussed the different methods you can use when delivering a speech and the importance of preparing properly. Despite completing both these objectives, you may one day find that your mind goes blank, you forget to bring a prop, or you encounter some other problem during your presentation. Here are examples and stories of real events gleaned from my membership in the National Speakers Association and how these professionals handled the situations.

You Get Sidetracked in the Middle of the Talk

There are three main reasons you may get sidetracked:

- You don't have clear objectives.
- You're not well prepared.
- You get irrelevant questions.

To Prevent It from Happening

Your objectives are crystal clear if you

- firmly establish your exact mission.
- develop a theme to support your mission.
- simplify your presentation to three or four main points to support the mission.
- make the "track" easy to follow, to help your audience follow your message.
- rehearse, rehearse, rehearse.

What to Do

Here are responses from successful speakers when they are asked irrelevant questions from the audience.

1. Answer the question briefly with respect and compassion for your audience. Remember, your audience is your customer. Treat the attendees with care.
2. Quickly tie the seemingly irrelevant question back into your topic.

When you find yourself getting sidetracked, check how much time you have left in your presentation. If there's a scheduled break, use the time to go over the presentation and decide what to cut or skip the break or create a *really* short break to compose yourself and ultimately save time.

(Tip provided by Lilly Walters, author of *Secrets of Successful Speakers,* McGraw-Hill, Inc., 1993.)

You Realize the Speaker Before You Has Already Told Your Story

For example, I had the opportunity to attend a presentation Jeff Dewar was giving to Lockheed Corporation at its Los Angeles headquarters when he was presenting his famous statistics speech, "What Does 99.9 Percent Quality Mean to You?" He introduced several themed scenarios—how often we drink contaminated water, how efficiently the normal heart operates, and so on—then went on to say that if any of those scenarios were to function at a 99.9 percent level of quality, it would mean, for example, "you would be drinking unsafe water for one hour each month," "your heart would fail to beat thirty-two thousand times a year," "some twenty-two thousand checks would be deducted from the wrong bank account each day," and so forth. Usually this part of his talk is a big hit, but at Lockheed that day it fell flat.

One of the attendees told Jeff afterward, "Sure seems like everybody is quoting from those 99.9 percent statistics."

Swelling with pride, Jeff said, "Really? And where did you hear them before?"

"Oh, the speaker this morning. He said *he* came up with them."

Not fun.

What to Do

- Watch and feel the audience. If you see people looking slyly at one another, chances are something is wrong.
- Casually stop, keep the mood you are trying to create in your tone of voice and mannerisms, and ask, "Have you heard this before?"
- Let the audience tell you. Turn it into a group sharing moment. Encourage your audience to tell you what an

earlier speaker said, then have them relate what they learned.

- Do not say anything about the other presenter using your material, unless you deliver it as a compliment!

You Trip on the Way to the Lectern

Even though you think you're walking with care, your mind might be on your presentation, and you trip.

To Prevent It from Happening

Before you stand up to walk to the lectern:

- Take a deep breath.
- Stand up and walk.
- Go slowly. Adrenaline is pumping through your system. Although you feel as if you're crawling to the lectern, your audience is seeing you scurry along at a good clip.

What to Do

First of all, know that the audience doesn't care that you tripped. However, they care if you get hurt, and they care if you make a scene about it.

- Make a lighthearted remark about your stumble, and it will more than likely set the stage for a great presentation. An audience likes you better when you demonstrate that you have faults—especially if you are able to laugh at your own shortcomings or flub-ups.

Here is a list of one-liners that can help you gloss over an embarrassing moment.

- I also do magic tricks.
- It took years of finishing school to learn to do that.

- I'm the only speaker who can fall up a set of steps.
- Is there a doctor in the house?
- All that money I spent at Arthur Murray's was a waste.
- I used to be too humble to stumble.
- Give me an inch and I'll take a fall.

(From *One-Liners for Disasters,* by Tom Antion, Anchor Publishing, 1993.)

Sample Speech: The Ceremonial

A ceremonial speech, also called a "testimonial speech," is given to honor a person or organization for something he or she has accomplished. For example, I gave the following speech, "Saying Good-Bye," during a snowstorm four years ago. I was honoring a fellow colleague who was retiring.

> *Ladies and gentlemen, we are here today to honor a distinguished colleague of ours for his dedicated years of service to this company. Tom has been not only a colleague of mine, but also a friend. Tom and I go way back. In fact, we go so far back, they had to use old-fashioned dating techniques to verify Tom's age. (Ha, ha.)*
>
> *Tom has been with us for more than twenty years and has finally decided to retire. We are going to miss him dearly. Tom is only retiring from work, not from life. Tom is only beginning a new phase of life. I am so glad to see all of you who weathered the winter storm out there just to touch base with Tom before he moves on to better, bigger, and more exciting things.*

This speech was effective because I added humor and touched upon Tom's accomplishments and what he meant to the company.

Tip of the Day

One of the most important rules to follow on the day of your speech is to not radically change your normal schedule. Get plenty of rest the night before. When you wake up the next day, have a nutritious, well-balanced breakfast. A healthy breakfast gives you the physical and mental energy you need for the speaking engagement. More than likely you are nervous, and nervousness requires energy. Your body needs food to give you energy. The best food to eat is whole-grain cereals, fruit, toast, and bagels with a glass of juice. Do not eat a heavy meal like eggs and bacon.

In Day 8 I will discuss special techniques to help you polish your speaking skills.

Day 8

Special Techniques

In this chapter I will discuss a variety of special techniques to help you develop and hone your speaking skills.

Also, I will provide you with an inside look at techniques I and other professional speakers use. By the end of this chapter you will know how to apply these ideas and tips to your presentation. Before you move forward with today's lessons, remember two things: First, the key is to use these techniques consistently. Second, public speaking is an acquired skill, and what you do before your presentation determines your success.

In order to incorporate special techniques, you will need to review your body language, movement, gestures, tone of voice, and overall performance.

Videotaping Yourself

Here is a general plan of all the different aspects of speech giving you can critique with the four-step analysis. At certain times you may wish to use all of these video techniques—at others only one or two may be necessary. Once you are familiar with the process, you can use your own judgment depending on the speech situation. Here is a list of elements to look for when reviewing your videotape:

- Posture
- Gestures
- Body movement
- Facial expressions
- Eye contact
- Voice

Remember, the first step in eliminating any superfluous mannerisms or language is to get an accurate perception of your body language and voice. Sit with a notepad and write down everything you notice on the video about your body language and voice.

- **Review #1.** Review the tape without looking for particular mannerisms. Just listen to the presentation as if you were hearing it for the first time and evaluate the *overall impact* you experience from watching the tape. During this initial review, pretend you are a member of the audience and evaluate your reaction to the presentation, trying to separate the fact that you are watching yourself. This will be difficult. Here are a few questions to think about and ask yourself during this review.

  —Did I like the presentation?

  —Was it informative or entertaining?

  —Would I recommend someone else watch this video?

- **Review #2.** Turn off the sound and look only for *visual distractions.* Jot down notes on what you observe. Make two lists, one for the things you liked and another for the things you did not like. Don't worry if your list of cons is longer; each time you give a presentation your performance will improve. Look specifically for the following:

—What did you do with your hands?

—What were your facial expressions?

—What did you do with your body?

—Did you move around? Did you stand still?

—Were there any mannerisms you found distracting or annoying?

—Did you seem appropriately animated?

- **Review #3.** Darken the picture or turn your back to the TV so you cannot see yourself and listen only to your voice. Many people have never heard a taping of their own voice before except maybe on their answering machine. Become accustomed to listening to your voice. The first reaction I have had from most people when they hear themselves for the first time is, "That doesn't sound like me!" What happens is that when you hear your voice for the first time you are not hearing it from "inside" your head. While listening to your voice, focus on the following:

  —What do you like and not like about your voice?

  —How was the speed of your speaking? Was it too fast or too slow?

  —How was your tone of voice?

  —How was your pitch? Was it too high or too low?

- **Review #4.** After you have completed your list of pros and cons, ask one or two family members to watch the tape with you. Get their initial impression. Have them take their own notes, and when the tape is finished compare your notes. Keep this list handy and tackle each negative point one at a time. And remember the positive ones!

Another important step is to gather all the notes and make another list. This is a list of those areas you believe need improvement. Make sure you are as specific as possible. Now take the items on the list and break them down into the following categories:

- **Voice and tone.** This includes the tone of your voice, speed, pitch, and any verbal distractions such as uhms, uhs, ers, and ya knows.
- **Nonverbal actions.** List them specifically by the parts of your body such as your hands, facial expressions, legs, arms, walking patterns, and so on. Don't be surprised if the list is long. That's okay. All novice speakers will have a long list when they first begin giving presentations. With practice, practice, and more practice, you eventually will see fewer areas in need of improvement. Look at the list and prioritize what areas you want to start working on immediately.

Make a conscious note of these areas and observe and listen to how you speak during your everyday activities. The next time you are at a party, business meeting, or with a friend see if you notice any of these distracting mannerisms. Also, do you notice any of these distractions while talking on the telephone?

Each time you speak, make an effort to eliminate or replace the distracting mannerism with a verbal or nonverbal technique. Practice every day. By making adjustments and changes in your everyday speaking style, you will find it easier to apply these strategies to your more formal speaking engagements such as a presentation at work, a toast at a wedding, or a speech to a large group.

Another helpful tip is to keep a journal after each presentation. Take a few moments to reflect on your speech. Make notes about your strengths and weaknesses and write a brief summary on your speech topic, the audience, and any other factors that will come in handy for future presentations.

Visualization: Self-Talk

One of the most effective techniques that I use myself and teach people in my seminars, workshops, and especially private coaching is visualization. Visualization is strongly tied to your own "self-talk." Self-talk is the conversation you have with yourself either in your head or out loud. If your self-talk is negative, destructive, or even invalid, your subconscious automatically accepts what you tell it. It doesn't say, *Oh, that was inappropriate, you don't want that.* Your mind records what you tell it, good or bad. It is imperative that you control your self-talk or it will control you. If you continue to have negative thoughts about yourself, you will sabotage any potential you have as a public speaker. Instead use positive self-talk: I can do this.

When you start to visualize yourself as a success, you will succeed.

The self-talk concept is the ability to relate or tie together your real performance as a speaker with your self-image as a speaker. This also relates directly back to your beliefs regarding speaking anxiety. Remember, it starts with what you call it and what you believe, right or wrong.

Consider the pattern of a speaker who is not confident with his or her speaking ability. This speaker goes into the situation totally unprepared, hoping it will be different, expecting the worst. And when you expect the worst, that's exactly what happens. Next thing you know, you hear yourself saying, *See, I told you you would fail.*

Let's take a look at a different approach. Imagine you said to yourself, I am looking forward to this presentation because I know I put a lot of time and effort into it and I will succeed because I am prepared! You would be amazed how this thinking creates positive, confident results.

Visualize yourself walking to the podium, stage, or lectern with confidence. The audience is listening to every word you are saying, glued to your next comment, and raising their hands because they want to hear more and ask interesting thought-provoking questions. If you start visualizing yourself as a success, over time you will see an improvement in your speaking style.

Say It Out Loud

The visualization process I just discussed is a powerful technique. However, rehearsing your presentation verbally, mentally, and physically is a key element to your success as a public speaker. If you want to "fine-tune" your body mentally and physically to a point where your mind and body are in sync, you need to act out your presentation. For example, I tell my clients to say their speech out loud while they're in the gym, taking a walk, preparing dinner, or driving in the car. This technique does three things:

- It forces you to engage your mind *and* your mouth at the same time. Your mind is a funny thing. On occasion when you start to say something out loud, you find that your mouth takes over what you intended to say and what comes out surprises even you.

- When your speech or presentation is completely planned, find a room where you can say your speech out loud. For example, if you are speaking at school, try to find a classroom that is not being used. If you are speaking at a corporation, see if there is a conference room or lounge where you can have privacy.
- Speak in the tone of voice, pitch, and volume you plan to use during the actual presentation.

Lessons from Mom: Be Yourself

I remember whenever I was assigned to tell a story in school, the night before, my mother would say to me, "Len, don't worry about what people think and how perfect you have to be, just *be yourself,* and tell your story." The best way to incorporate Mom's advice is to visualize and relive the event. As a speaker, when you focus on communicating with your audience and sharing ideas as opposed to focusing on your performance, the speaking process becomes easier. Don't start your presentation thinking, I wonder if they will like my presentation, or, I hope they don't think I am lousy, or, Oh no, they probably know more than I do and will be bored. All too often this negative self-talk is a major source of speech anxiety.

You are your own worst enemy, and the sooner you think more positively and trust in your abilities because you did prepare, the sooner you'll realize the powerful role your thought process plays in your success as a speaker. When you tell any story, the best technique is to relate something personal for your audience. In addition, you need to act out your story for your audience. This is where facial expressions and gestures come in handy. In this situation it's perfectly normal to exaggerate your gestures to drive your point home.

Type of Speech: Demonstrative

A demonstration speech is similar to an informative speech, except you tell the audience how to do something. For a sample demonstration speech, I have decided to demonstrate how to organize your thoughts and ideas for your speeches. You will find this demonstration an integral part of organizing your presentation. This is an excerpt from a speech called "Mind Mapping" that I have taught to numerous clients. I have been using this technique for almost thirty years not only to deliver speeches, but to write articles and books.

> *Take a single sheet of paper and draw a circle in the center of the paper. This is reserved for your speech title. Let's assume your speech has four main points. Draw four lines branching off from the circle in the center of the page. Each branch represents a main idea of your speech. Now draw two lines off each main idea branch. These lines are reserved for your key points. Label each one of your main idea lines with what you will discuss first, second, and so on. From each main idea, label the key point lines as "a" and "b" to indicate which point comes first. Once you have filled in all the lines, your speech is mapped out.*
>
> *The goal of this method is to get your ideas down on paper in an organized manner to help you deliver your speech.*

The After-Dinner Speech

This is an example of another type of speech you may be asked to give someday. There are several kinds of after-dinner speeches. The specific topic of an after-dinner speech varies according to the event but usually focuses on saying a few words of wisdom and encouragement, often to motivate people and leave them with a pleasant impression of the event.

Here is an example of an after-dinner speech I gave to a large international sales force at the end of a four-day weekend of training. The company that hired me wanted me to motivate and inspire the attendees to use the presentation skills and training they had acquired over the weekend and apply them in their work environment. This is an abridged version of the speech, "The Motivation to I.N.S.P.I.R.E."

> *When you are asked to think about what the word "inspire" means to you, you may not come up with the same meaning as the person sitting next to you. If I were to ask each of you in this room to define the word "inspire," we would get several variations as to the meaning. Here is my definition of inspire: "to have the ability to change attitudes." Your attitude will not change until someone motivates or inspires you to think differently, and that is what I am here to talk about tonight. I have devised an acronym for the word* inspire. *Using this acronym, I will tell you how you can apply the techniques you learned this weekend to your next presentation.*

- I *stands for the word* influence. *As world-class salespeople and now world-class presenters, you have the opportunity to influence many people. Think about what your next goal is as a speaker. Is it to influence a buyer? Is it to influence a partner, or is it to influence or impress your boss?*

  Whatever your goal is, rest assured, you will *make an impression and you will influence people to think, but will you influence them to think correctly?*

- N *stands for the word* need. *To be successful in all your speeches, you must fully understand and address your audience's needs. For example, does my audience need to know every statistic on the health care reform? Will my audience need another visual aid to get my point? Am I belaboring one point for too long?*

- S *stands for the word* success. *Stanford University conducted a study several years ago with successful salespeople, and here is what they found:*
    - *Preparation accounts for 75 percent of your presentation.*
    - *Breathing accounts for 15 percent of your presentation.*
    - *Mental focus accounts for 10 percent of your presentation.*

What does this mean? The study proves that 75 percent of your success as a speaker depends heavily on your preparation. In order to achieve success, you need to properly prepare and implement your ideas.

- P *stands for the word* passion. *You must have passion for your subject or you won't inspire anyone. At the same time, just being passionate about your topic will not guarantee success.* P *can also stand for* preparation. *Proper preparation, coupled with using a personal story, is an effective tool for inspiring your audience.*
- I *stands for the word* improve. *You will not improve unless you practice, practice, practice. Practice what you learned over the last four days of this conference. Remember, practice is the key to improving.*
- R *stands for the word* rewards. *You will find that when you do practice and rehearse the skills you have learned over the last several days, you are rewarded with a better presentation. In turn you will be a more effective salesperson.*

- E *stands for the word* enthusiasm. *I hope that this weekend has been an opportunity for you to learn, grow, and get enthused about giving presentations. Take your enthusiasm and channel that energy back into your presentations and you will inspire and motivate yourself and the audience you are addressing.*

Tip of the Day

Go back to Day 1, when I told you to keep a list of categories for your speech topics. It's time to tap into your memory bank and write a story for each category. Don't worry about when you will use the story, just recall and collect the details for later use. Write out each story in longhand or type it on your computer. Let your creative juices flow. Try to remember everything possible about the category. Keep the stories conversational. Think back to your childhood, teenage years, times you were sick or hurt, vacations, neighbors, friends, even your pets. You can also include stories and funny anecdotes about your work life, career success, and travel. When you have completed these stories you will have a database of jokes, anecdotes, advice, and thought-provoking questions you can integrate into your speeches. Take the time to review and reflect on your past speeches and see where you could have used a personal story.

In Day 9 I will discuss additional methods you can use to psych yourself up and deliver the best presentation.

Day 9

Behind the Scenes

Building Confidence

Your speech, props, and visual aids are ready. Now comes the final part of planning a speech or presentation—mental preparation. In order to deliver the best speech or presentation, you have to "psych" yourself up for the big moment. In this chapter I show you how to achieve this goal. Throughout the chapter I've sprinkled tips and strategies to show you how to become your own best coach, the importance of making a checklist, and a refresher lesson on the dos and don'ts of public speaking. In addition, you will learn how to deliver a persuasive speech—and for an added bonus, I teach you how to deliver bad news or negative results in a speech.

Becoming Your Own Best Coach

Although you've gotten feedback from family and friends on your speeches, ultimately you are responsible for coaching yourself through the speech process. Since your mind is a powerful machine, your body reacts to what your mind suggests. *You* are your own best coach. Your thoughts, either positive or negative, determine the success of your presentation. Therefore you need to continually strive for greatness in your speeches or presentations. If you have children or ever played a sport yourself, you know how exhilarating it is when a coach praises the team for a job well done. In public speaking you are not only the coach, but the team. It all rests on your shoulders. As your own coach, tell yourself every day that you are a winner in public speaking. Every day practice your techniques and strategies so you're ready for your next big speech.

The Importance of Checklists

Go the extra mile to make sure your speech or presentation is a grand slam. I make checklists for every presentation, seminar, or workshop I give. Since any one of a host of problems can sabotage your presentation, it is imperative that you not let the little things fall by the wayside. In my career as a public speaker, I have spoken at many conventions and conferences and witnessed presenters panic because they forgot their visual aids, can't find their handouts, or didn't get the name of the individual coordinating the meeting or the new location of the hotel or meeting center when it was changed at the last minute.

These are mistakes that can frazzle your nerves. To prevent this from happening to you, here are examples of checklists I use.

The Prespeech Checklist

Use this checklist when you are planning to give a speech to an association or organization. "The sooner the better" is the motto you should follow when you are putting together your prespeech checklist. As the date of your presentation draws closer, make sure to confirm the following points.

- **The actual date and time of the speech.** Make sure the date and time of your speech is the same as when you sent the information to the meeting planner along with your precustom survey. Over the years I have experienced several occasions when the date and time have changed, especially when I wasn't the only speaker on the program. However, even if you are the only speaker on the program, contact the hotel or convention center at least one week prior to your presentation to make sure the date and time are accurate.

  Let me share a story of when a presenter didn't confirm the date and time. My colleague was scheduled to speak to a large crowd at an association meeting in June. He did not call or contact the organizer after the date was scheduled. The day before the scheduled presentation, he flew into the city where he was speaking. When he arrived at the hotel he asked if anyone else from the association had registered yet. When the hotel checked the reservations list, they told him they had no record of that association being scheduled to speak at the hotel. Naturally he was confused, and after several phone calls to members of the association he quickly learned that he had made a huge mistake. Yes, he was at the hotel on the correct date, but he had arrived a year early!

  Keep in mind that many associations schedule their meetings two or three years in advance, and it is not unusual for them to book speakers for the events at that same time. When he was contacted in March, my colleague had written down the date of the speech for the upcoming June. Since he thought the presentation was only a few months away and he was never contacted again by the association, he assumed everything was all set. Boy, did he get a very expensive surprise!

This story illustrates the necessity of confirming all dates, times, and locations. Once again, never assume anything when you are planning a speech or presentation.

- **Prepare enough copies of your handouts.** Confirm the number of people attending your session. Either bring extra copies with you or make arrangements with the hotel or convention center to have the copies ready when you arrive. If you choose the latter route, send copies of your materials to the appropriate person at least a week prior to the event. Include a cover letter asking the hotel to hold the materials for you for the particular date. Call to follow up that the package arrived, and get the name of a contact person. Always put yourself in the audience's mind. I have attended seminars where there were not enough handouts. I felt cheated, and it did not leave a good first impression with me. When I'm the speaker, I call the day before to confirm the number of attendees and add a few extra copies just in case additional people decide to show up. Associations such as the New England Speakers Association conduct monthly meetings and always have walk-in registrations. Walk-ins can account for 30 percent of your attendance. I always take that factor into account and bring 30–50 percent more copies. Also, there will be times when your session runs concurrently with other sessions and participants may want a handout even though they cannot attend your presentation. To accommodate them, leave extra copies at the back of the room.

- **Make a packing list.** Make a list of everything you need to bring with you for the presentation. I advise doing this at least three days before the speaking engagement. Check each item off the list as you pack it. In doing this, you know everything is packed and ready to go and you won't panic on the day of the presentation. Bring a copy of the checklist with you. When you unpack you can check that everything made it into the box. If you are driving yourself to the presentation, load the materials into your car the day before. If you are flying to the location, have the seminar materials shipped to the location at least one week ahead of time, so in the event the boxes are misplaced or lost, there is time to track the shipment. Always send a tracking slip with the shipment and keep a copy for your records. Very important! If you are sending materials to a hotel, call the hotel and ask where shipments are stored and with whom you should speak to confirm their arrival.
- **Call one more time.** On the day or evening before your presentation, call your contact person, meeting planner, or hotel staff member to confirm that there have been no changes, such as room location or starting time of your speech. It is not unusual for times and locations to change at the last minute. For example, I was hired as a speaker for an association meeting where the number of people who registered was higher than originally expected and the location was changed to accommodate a larger group. When you arrive at the hotel, double-check one more time. Also, if the number of attendees has greatly increased beyond the 30–50 percent you anticipate, have additional copies of your materials

made. If the hotel or convention center can't do it for you, ask if there is a local photocopy center nearby so you can arrange to have more copies made in plenty of time.

Speech Day Checklist

There are several tasks you can complete to ensure that you are properly prepared on the day of your speech.

- **Arrive early.** Arrive early so you have time to unwind, find the room location, and check its setup. Although you provided a room layout in the earlier stages of your speech planning, it doesn't hurt to check, double-check, or even triple-check.

  For many of my presentations, I arrive the evening before and take care of the room setup that night. If possible, arrange to meet with someone from the organization staff and have dinner together. This gives you the chance to get to know him or her and review any last minute requests you have.

  For example, I can remember a speaking engagement where I was the closing keynote speaker for a week of training conducted for an international sales force. Some of these presenters were, not to my surprise, still making last minute changes to their presentations. They were monopolizing a room of computers that had been set up especially for the training week.

  As I walked around the room and introduced myself to some of the presenters, it became clear to me that they were in a panic. What happened was that a computer virus had infected the networked computers and many of the speakers had lost their presentation slides and were scrambling to duplicate them. During my conversations with the speakers, I also learned that about 25 percent were named Mike. Arriving the night before paid off. I incorporated these two facts (computer virus and the name Mike) into my keynote speech the next day. I was a hit. Arriving early allowed me to further customize my presentation at the last minute.

- **Contact your liaison for the event.** When you arrive, contact the person who hired you. Ask if he or she would like to meet you in the room where you are speaking to check over the details and any last-minute changes.
- **Unpack.** As you unpack and set up your materials for your session, make sure you place your materials where they are accessible to you. Use your packing list to check off each item as you take care of it. Place handouts at the back of the room or wherever you deem logical.
- **Arrange for a pitcher of warm water.** Arrange to have a pitcher and glass of warm water nearby. Drinking warm water not only helps wet your mouth, but also relaxes your vocal cords and muscles. Contrary to popular belief, drinking ice water only tightens up your voice muscles. Inquire with the hotel staff or meeting planner if you need an extra table for the pitcher and glass, especially if you are speaking from a lectern.
- **Check out your equipment.** The last thing you do is check out your equipment. Make sure you have spare bulbs for the overhead projector if you are using one. Test out your writing implements to make sure they still work. Make sure your equipment does not obstruct the audience's view from any part of the room and that they can see you and your visual aids from where they are sitting.

Hopefully you can now relax before your speech or presentation; knowing that everything is in place, you can psych yourself up for the actual event. It is very hard to get pumped up if you are worrying about last minute details.

Meet and Greet

Again, arrive early to meet and greet as many participants as possible before your presentation. If there is a cocktail hour or a meet-and-greet session, make an effort to introduce yourself to as many people as you can before the program. Get to know as many of their names as possible and even go so far as to ask them what they are expecting during your presentation.

These techniques allow you to listen to your audience's expectations and may remind you of personal stories you can incorporate into your presentation that relate to issues they bring up. Do not limit yourself to meeting and speaking only with the leaders of the organization, association, or company; get to know participants and their guests as well.

Do not consume alcohol during the social hour. I avoid alcoholic beverages before I speak since it can affect my presentation. Hold your beverage in your left hand so your right hand is free to shake hands with people as you greet them.

Top Ten List: The Ultimate Dos and Don'ts List

Let's take a moment to review what you should and shouldn't do during your presentation.

1. Don't underestimate the time it takes to prepare a presentation.
2. Don't wait until the night before to put your presentation together.
3. Do prepare and rehearse your presentation.
4. Don't stay up all night worrying about your presentation.
5. Do double-check spelling on your visual aids.
6. Do drink lots of water to protect your speaking voice.
7. Do arrive early to properly set up for your presentation.
8. Do meet and greet as many people as you can before you speak.
9. Don't drink alcohol. This may affect your presentation.
10. Don't ever apologize for being nervous.

Types of Speeches: Persuasive

In a persuasive speech you are persuading the audience to make a change, such as how they think about conflict, or getting the audience to do something they do not do now. Here is an example of a persuasive speech—"Why Join Toastmasters International"—that I give during workshops and seminars.

Why Join Toastmasters International

Whatever your personal and professional goals are in life, your success depends on your ability to communicate effectively. If you learn to express yourself and your ideas in a clear and concise manner so you are heard, understood, and respected, then you possess the qualities of a leader.

Where can you go to obtain the necessary support and training to further develop your speaking skills? Wouldn't it be great to belong to an organization that helps you improve your speaking skills? Wouldn't you love to have someone provide you with positive and constructive feedback? You bet!

For the last several years, I have been a member of Toastmasters International, an organization formed in 1924 specifically for this purpose. In fact, the organization has more than 170,000 members from a variety of occupations and backgrounds. This organization is not just for professional speakers, it is for everyone! *Toastmasters International was founded by Dr. Ralph C. Smedley, who conceived and developed the idea of helping others speak more effectively and with more confidence. More clubs were formed, and Toastmasters International was incorporated under California law in December 1932.*

I hold the highest rank in the organization, Distinguished Toastmasters Designation (DTM). This achievement took years of dedication, service, and hard work but was well worth the effort. This program benefits more than three million people worldwide, and you can be the next member. The benefits you gain as a member can change your life. As a Toastmaster, you learn how to overcome the initial nervousness you feel when called upon to give a speech or presentation. You learn how to logically organize and present your ideas with conviction. You also learn how to improve your ability to listen to other people's ideas and evaluate them with constructive criticism. The confidence you gain shows not only in your formal presentations, but also in your everyday speaking situations.

Toastmasters is a nonprofit organization, and the yearly membership fee is less than $100. There is an initial $16 new membership fee, along with $18 dues every six months plus any local club dues to cover expenses. This total is less than many one-day seminars you may have attended.

Being a member of Toastmasters also helps you learn how to become a team leader and conduct meetings more effectively. Many of you, I'm sure, possess some of these skills already. Toastmasters only enhances them.

Here is how Toastmasters works. Toastmaster organizations are either open to the public, referred to as "open club," or associated with a specific organization or company and restrict their membership to only employees, "closed club." Toastmaster groups meet weekly, monthly, or bimonthly. At these meetings, a group of twenty or more people meet for an hour to two hours, depending on the club. Each meeting provides members an opportunity to practice their speaking skills, whether it is running the meeting or serving as one of the scheduled speakers on the program for that meeting. Furthermore, there are other speaking opportunities for everyone in attendance. At the same time, you have fun, and without realizing it, you are improving your speaking skills. Each member receives a variety of manuals and resources along with access to videotapes and audiotapes on public speaking and leadership skills. In addition, you have access to some of the best resources you can find—its members. Every member has the same goal—to become a more effective speaker—and Toastmasters provides you with a format that has a proven track record.

I'm sure many of you are members of an association, school, or church committee where you are required to make presentations or speeches. Toastmasters helps you succeed in these roles as well. If you are anxious to improve quickly, you can. If you want to progress at a more leisurely pace, you can do that, too. Toastmasters is not a classroom; rather, it is a workshop for you to develop your communication and leadership skills among friends. Not convinced? Visit any Toastmasters meeting as a guest and see for yourself. You only need to find a club near you, find out when and where they meet, and show up.

Becoming a member of Toastmasters is easy. There is probably a Toastmasters Club meeting in your town or a neighboring town. To locate a Toastmasters club near you and find more information, visit their Web site at www.toastmasters.org, or call them at 800-993-7732 to request information by mail.

I can say truthfully, if it wasn't for Toastmasters, I would not be a professional speaker today. I also know that without the experiences I gained from Toastmasters, I would not have developed and honed my speaking skills. So here is your call to action.

This persuasive speech was a success because I told the audience about the numerous benefits of the program and asked thought-provoking questions, getting them to evaluate their own speaking skills.

Types of Speeches: Reporting on Negative Results or Bad News

One of the most difficult speeches to give is one in which you are required to deliver bad news or negative results. Often this type of speech is given by a person lower in an organization who needs to inform the higher-ups of a problem. The best approach when faced with this challenge is to prepare a presentation containing the pertinent details and facts. Above all, the best advice is to let the facts speak for themselves.

In my former engineering career, I often had to make a presentation about a project that was not going as planned, and I had to consider whether obtaining more information or changing direction was the way to go. Let's review the general format to use in this instance, and then I will give an example using these guidelines.

The objectives of most presentations that involve negative or bad news is to

- inform the management of specific events, results, or issues.
- make recommendations.
- get support and direction from management.

In some cases specific recommendations are unknown until you are advised by upper management. However, in my experience, if you identify a problem and give recommendations as to what *you* would do, it is easier for management to endorse the solution or indicate that they want to study the results and make their own recommendations. In most cases they welcome the fact that you took the initiative to come up with solutions.

Here's an example of a time when I had to inform management of an engineering analysis I just completed.

Someone had indicated to management that a materials engineering review was not performed and they needed the review and approval of a design before installation. I was approached, and after reviewing the data test results for about two weeks, I realized that there were problems with the current design because improper materials were used. I was under the gun to complete this review and found myself pressured to approve the design. I knew that what I was going to tell management would not be considered good news, since it would mean a delay in the completion of the project. However, it was more important for management to know all the facts so they could make the final decision. I requested that I have an opportunity to make a presentation to management and explain my findings and results. Here's the structure I used for the meeting.

- I presented an overview of the objectives of the engineering review and study, including the desired results of the review—approval of the material selection.
- I described what I specifically reviewed and analyzed and against what criteria. I defined what was and wasn't acceptable regarding the results.
- I pointed out where the test results were not what I would expect. I discussed why the test failures were significant and what the consequences meant in terms of the design. In this case, the materials needed to be

replaced with the appropriate ones, and I gave specific recommendations to correct the problem.

- I outlined the various options I would pursue were I the decision maker and stated my recommendations as to the approach to take, along with the risks involved if other alternatives were considered. Since cost was a big factor, I included a detailed cost analysis for each option.
- I indicated the preferred option and what was needed to implement it, along with a schedule. This option would delay the project by several weeks. I also described what I believed was the next best option, again with the cost schedule.

Management will likely support you either way. In my case, I found some additional ways to expedite the schedule and replace the components. In the end, the project did not lose a significant amount of time. Later, upper management sent me a memo thanking me for being so thorough and honest and for allowing them to have a part in the decision.

To sum up what you do in situations like the one I just shared:

- Provide all the facts.
- Do not lay blame on anyone.
- Provide specific recommendations.

Tip of the Day

In order to prepare yourself a few minutes before your speaking engagement, many presenters have a routine they follow to psych themselves up for their speech. Here is an example of a presenter who got himself so psyched about his speech that he didn't know what room he was in.

The gentleman was pacing back and forth, reviewing his notes in the hotel hallway outside the room where he was speaking. As more participants arrived, he decided he did not want everyone to see him pacing back and forth nervously, so he ducked into another room off the hallway. He began practicing his opening statement and how he would walk to the lectern as he was introduced. He was really getting into it.

After about five minutes of rehearsal a woman came up to him and said, "Oh, you must be our lunchtime speaker?"

"Yes," he replied.

The woman responded by saying, "I can see you are very nervous."

He replied, "Why do you say that?"

"Well," the woman responded, "why else would you be standing in the ladies' room!"

You have to give him credit—at least he *did* consider it important enough to do some last minute rehearsing.

His concept was great, but I would have chosen another location. Here is what I find works best for me. If I'm at a hotel for a speaking engagement, I take a walking tour of the entire hotel. As I walk, I visualize the presentation in my mind. I use the stairs and not the elevator to release as much nervous energy as possible. Generally I don't get nervous before a speech or presentation, but I find this routine helps to psych me up for the big moment. I stop in the men's room (please check the sign before entering), wash my face with cold water, and check that my hair is combed and my tie is straight. At that point I'm jazzed for my presentation and ready to go.

Find a routine that works best for you. It can be as simple as taking a walk or as outrageous as running around the parking lot, screaming, "I'm the greatest speaker ever!" The important thing is to get yourself charged up about your presentation.

Your enthusiasm comes across in your speech and is one of the main reasons your speech is a success.

In Day 10 I will discuss how to end your speech or presentation with a bang. In addition, I will show you how to prepare for the question and answer period following your speech.

Day 10

Ending Your Speech with a Bang

In this final chapter I focus on how to end your speech or presentation with a memorable conclusion, the most effective way to handle the question and answer segment following your speech or presentation, and how to deal with hostile questions from audience members without losing your composure. Finally, I share another type of speech you may be asked to give in the future—the impromptu speech.

Final Component

Throughout the book I've talked about the importance of your speech or presentation's structure—the introduction, body, and conclusion. All communication—a staff meeting, phone call, casual conversation, formal speech, and business presentation—must follow a logical order.

Would you call someone on the telephone and start off by saying good-bye? Of course not. Your conclusion needs to serve as a review of your message. It's 10 percent of your total presentation, regardless of its length. Audience members tend to remember the last words they hear you say, so it's vital that your key message or messages are restated in your conclusion.

In your conclusion, repeat the purpose of your presentation, summarize your key points, and give the audience a "call to action." It is important to tell participants what you want them to do with the information they learned as a result of your speech. However, in my career as a public speaker, I have heard many presenters begin their conclusion with the following phrases:

- "In conclusion . . ."
- "Let me summarize . . ."
- "Let me quickly review . . ."
- "In summary . . ."

The problem with this approach is that most audiences tune you out the second they hear these phrases. Remember this key phrase: "Don't say what you're going to say, just say it." Here are five methods and examples I use to keep my audience fastened to their seats as I end my presentation.

1. **Verbally list your points.** I use this method with one of my most requested keynote speeches, "The Seven Aspects of a Dynamic Presentation." At the conclusion, I review the seven aspects along with tips for each one. For example, I start off by saying, "As you can see, each of these seven aspects plays a key role in your presentations. Now let's quickly review each one of them again."
2. **Summarize your points.** When you are ready to summarize your points, highlight the introduction and body again.
3. **Tie it together.** As you put the finishing touches on your speech, make sure your presentation comes full

circle by relating your conclusion back to your introduction. For example, "When I began my session today I identified several objectives for this course. Let's go back and review these objectives and see how they all tie together."

4. **Refer to your purpose.** Every speech has a purpose, whether it's telling your audience how to build an object, persuading them to join a group or buy a product, or informing them about a specific piece of information. For example, "Remember the purpose of my presentation today was to demonstrate how proper preparation is the key to delivering a successful presentation."
5. **Close with a quote.** Closing with a quote leaves the audience with a visual image of your message. For example, when referring to the importance of preparation, I have closed many speeches with this quote: "Remember, the willingness to win is worth nothing unless you have the willingness to prepare, so prepare, prepare, prepare."

Although your conclusion is short, its significance is important. This is your last chance to drive your message home and leave a lasting impression.

In some instances I combine my closing remarks or statements with a theatrical closing, one that involves props or even a costume. When I do this, each time an audience member picks up that object they are reminded of my presentation. Here is one example of an occasion where I used costume and props.

In Day 3 I discussed a motivational speech I gave to a sales force at Mt. Snow in New England. Since the setting was a ski lodge, I thought it would be effective to provide a more dramatic closing, one the group would remember but also one that would drive the message home. I asked, "How many in the group can relate the ability to speak on their feet to skiing down a mountain?" I then donned a pair of ski goggles and talked about the importance of wearing your goggles. Next came a funny-looking ski hat with bells on it, and I talked about the importance of a hat. I took a sheet of paper with the number *1* written on it and tied it around my neck, to simulate that I was in a competition. I then quickly asked the group, while pointing to the *1*, if they would pick anything different. Finally I put on my ski gloves and positioned myself as if I were ready to ski down the hill and said, "The perfect moment."

At this point in my closing, I'm standing in a business suit wearing ski goggles, a stupid-looking hat, gloves, and a racing number hanging from around my neck, and the audience is laughing hysterically. I then use these props to compare speaking with skiing.

> *Picture yourself facing down the hill (the hill of speaking), and as you start off, you fall. What do you do? You pick yourself up and start again. How many of you have tried to give a speech and failed? What did* you *do? You try it again.*
>
> *You start down the hill, and again you fall. You look around to see if anyone saw your blunder, and a little kid skis by and says, "Hi, Dad." Once again, you pick yourself up, and after a few practice runs, you stop falling. Later that day you feel more confident, so you say to yourself, I don't need these gloves, and you remove the gloves. A little while later you decide you no longer need the goggles, and off they go. You soon realize it's not as cold out as you thought and you don't need the hat. Why? Because "you're number one."*
>
> *At this point I rip off the paper sign and hold it up.*

You may be asking how this helps with closing a speech. Here's how. As a public speaker, you face your own speaking challenges, and as you attempt to go down bigger and more challenging hills, remember one thing: Just because you fall down does not mean you are not facing in the right direction. The more you go down that hill, the better you become. The same occurs when you give a speech or presentation.

Treat each speaking opportunity as a downhill race. Sometimes you fall and sometimes you don't, but remember, get back up (speaking, that is) and try it again until your confidence has you winning the race.

Here is why this is an example of an effective speech conclusion. Not only did I compare skiing to speaking, but I used actual ski equipment as the method to "paint a vivid picture" in the participants' minds, one they won't forget.

Q&A: Fielding Questions from Your Audience

Many presenters dread participating in a question and answer (Q&A) period following their presentation. I, on the other hand, look forward to a good Q&A session. It is during these periods of exchange that the audience has the opportunity to ask questions about my topic.

To prepare yourself for the Q&A session, let's review eight steps.

1. **Listen to the entire question.** Too many speakers do *not* take the time to really listen to the question. Sometimes they start answering the question even before the participant finishes asking it. If you don't listen to the entire question, you won't give the appropriate response.
2. **Repeat the question for the audience.** To ensure you correctly heard and understood the question, repeat it for the audience. This approach accomplishes three things. First, it makes sure everyone in the audience

heard the question. I'm sure you remember a time when you attended a Q&A session and didn't hear the question. Instead all you heard was the speaker's answer, since he or she was miked. Second, repeating the question allows you additional time to evaluate the question and plan your answer. Finally, should you misunderstand the question, this gives the participant who originally asked the question an opportunity to correct you and repeat or rephrase it. Don't be afraid to ask a participant to be more specific with a question.

3. **Credit the person asking the question.** For example, you can say, "Thank you, that was a great question," or, "That is a question many people have asked me." You get the idea. One word of caution: When you do thank a participant for asking a question, make sure you extend the same courtesy to every member with a question.
4. **Give an honest answer.** If you do not know the answer to a particular question, don't lie or fabricate a false response. Be honest and say, "I'm sorry, I do not have an answer for that right now. May I get back to you on it?" If you are honest, your audience respects your candor and won't lose faith in your presentation. Make sure you get the name and phone number or e-mail address for the audience member you need to follow up with.
5. **Bridge to the next question.** After you answer a question, say to the participant who asked the question, "Did that answer your question?" or "Was that the type of information you were looking for?" Once an audience member gives you the nod and says, "Yes," this gives you permission to move on to the next person. Even if you don't completely answer the audience member's question, the fact that you received

permission to move on to another question shifts the responsibility away from you and back to the participant.

6. **Request that the participant stand.** By asking the participant who is asking the question to stand, you are able to see the person directing the question at you and you may deter a participant from pursuing a hostile approach with the question.
7. **Provide paper for questions.** Many people are not comfortable standing up and asking a question. They would much rather write down their question and let you read it. Offer the audience index cards and encourage them to write down their questions during the presentation or during a break.
8. **Write down the questions.** Have a pen handy to jot down questions in case you are unable to answer one or more and want to get back to the participant's question at another time. One word of caution: Do not tell a participant you will get back with an answer if you have no intention of doing so.

What If Nobody Asks a Question?

The silence at the end of your speech or presentation is deafening. You can avoid this silence or at least lessen the void by using the following strategies.

- **Take an informal survey.** For example, ask the audience, "How many of you came with different expectations about what you would get out of today's program?" "How many of you actually found that today's session provided the answers to your questions and more?"

- **Pose your own question.** Here's one way to create a question. Omit an obvious part of your speech, such as a statistic or solution to a problem. Then create a question in which you can present the information in the answer, such as "Do any of you know what the federal government says [or has done] about this issue?" Then go ahead and elaborate.
- **Select an audience member ahead of time to ask the first question.** Arrange with the meeting planner or event chairperson to select one participant to ask the first question (or do it him- or herself). This gets the ball rolling and helps the audience feel confident about posing questions.

How to Handle Hostile Questions

There are times when an audience is hostile or you anticipate tension following a presentation on a controversial issue. Here are strategies to use when dealing with hostile questions.

- **Listen to the entire question.** While listening to the question, try to identify the real issue the audience member is addressing.
- **Depersonalize the question.** Rephrase the question in a less hostile tone or within a more neutral context. For example, if a participant says, "What makes you an authority on unemployment?" you can depersonalize the question by rephrasing it: "Let me begin by telling you how long I was unemployed before becoming a public speaker."

- **Dissect.** Hostile questions often come in multiple parts. Break up the question or dissect it into parts by responding to the part of the question that is easiest for you.
- **Look at someone else in the audience.** This is the one time you do not have to maintain eye contact with the person asking the question. Here's why. Many people who ask hostile questions are seeking attention, and by not looking at them, you do not give them the satisfaction of knowing they've hit a nerve. Also, by speaking to the rest of the audience, you can focus on your side of the confrontation.

Often hostile questions spring from strictly black-and-white or for-or-against perspectives or attitudes. Your objective is to enable your audience to see the many shades of gray that exist with respect to most controversial issues. If you have built your presentation on solid facts, your message is even stronger once you have responded professionally to this confrontation. You need to have all the facts and figures ready for instant recall.

Top Ten List: Ways to Diffuse Hostility

Here is my list of the best ways to handle opposing viewpoints.

1. **Make certain you have been understood.** Restate your position so that it is clear in the audience's mind.
2. **Be poised.** Shift the focus from the point of conflict toward the more fundamental principles on which the group agrees. Help the audience agree with you on

principles and indisputable facts, and they will readily agree with you on points in the rest of your speech.

3. **Illustrate the common goals of the audience, the organization, or yourself.** Clarify the problem or argument from the audience's point of view. Change their view of the situation from a black-and-white standpoint to one that allows for shades of gray. Do this in a helpful, informative manner. Never become argumentative.
4. **Encourage your audience to look at all sides of an issue.** Many times when audience members feel negatively about a topic, they are focusing too strongly on isolated aspects of the issue. Using facts, statistics, quotes, and citations, encourage them to look at the issue from all sides. Use clear examples that the audience understands.
5. **Tactfully refute the opposition.** Counter the opposition's arguments that already have convinced your audience. Do it in a nonthreatening manner. Avoid statements that may be interpreted as a personal attack on your audience or their association. Illustrate ways in which adopting your viewpoint is more helpful to them personally than if they choose to follow the opposition. In other words, appeal to their self-interest.
6. **Be truthful.** If you bend the truth, you almost always get caught. Play it straight, even if your position seems momentarily weakened.
7. **Be friendly.** Always control your temper. A calm, cool speaker creates an aura of confidence. When the participant is hostile, respond as though he or she were a friend. Any attempt to put down or belittle your

participant with sarcasm immediately draws the audience's sympathy away from you.

8. **Be fair.** Take questions from every side of the room. Don't limit yourself to front rows, and don't let one person monopolize your time. Ask the audience, "Does anyone else have something to say on this subject?"
9. **Watch your body language.** Don't place your hands on your hips or point at the audience. Both of these are scolding poses, and they give you the appearance of preaching.
10. **Quit while you're ahead.** Don't exceed the allotted time. Keep an eye on a clock or have someone signal you. You have the power to close the presentation whenever you want.

Handling Challenging Questions

After my clients give a speech, I meet with them to review how their presentation went. One of the most important parts of this debriefing is to review how the Q&A portion proceeded, especially difficult to answer questions. Following are five such types of questions audience members may ask during a presentation.

1. **The question is off the topic.** There are times when you may be asked a question that is not related to your topic. If this happens, tell the audience member that you would be happy to discuss the questions after you finish your presentation. If it's related to a topic you will cover later in your presentation, tell the person you will review that topic shortly and ask him or her to wait until that point. Usually most audience members don't

have a problem. However, in some cases the person asking the question insists on getting an answer right away. I tell the person I have no problem taking the time now to answer the question, but I ask the audience how they feel about it. "Do you mind if I answer this gentleman's question now, or would you rather I wait until later?" With this approach the group, not me, decides. Depending on their response, I either address the question immediately or wait.

2. **An audience member asks an attacking question.** With any question that appears to attack you as a speaker, first and foremost, remain professional. Do not lash back at the person and attack or you will alienate yourself from the rest of the audience. Remember, the important thing is that people may not be attacking you personally but taking issue with your topic. Instead ask the person to repeat the question to make sure you understand what is being asked. By doing this, you are stalling for time so you can formulate a defense. Then rephrase the question in a less hostile manner and give your response. Here is one example that I have come across in my presentations: "What makes you such an expert on presentation skills?" When this happens I rephrase the question such as "You are probably wondering where I got all my speaking experience." I simply rephrased the question to a more positive tone.
3. **An audience member asks a question and you don't have the answer.** Occasionally there are times when you will not know the answer to a question. In these circumstances do not try to bluff your way through; the audience usually knows what you are doing. Instead tell the audience member you don't have the answer for that question and you will get back to him or her later with

an answer. Another option is to pose the question to the entire group. In some cases another audience member will know the answer, and the audience will appreciate your asking for their opinion.

4. **The audience member asks for proprietary information that you can't give out.** If someone asks you a proprietary question, simply respond by telling the person that the answer contains information you are not at liberty to discuss. However, if you have a resource or contact person who can answer the question, offer that information. Then ask if the person has another question. Giving the person the opportunity to ask another question prevents him or her from feeling ignored.
5. **The answer you give the audience is one you know they won't like.** You may find yourself in a situation where you must say things the audience won't like. Be honest and preface your response by telling the audience your answer may not make them happy. This shows that you are aware of your audience's feelings. Here is one example from my experience. A person in one of my seminars heard that the computer monitor had just failed. He says to me, "I hear that we won't be able to use the computer for our presentations this afternoon. I was really looking forward to learning how to use the new software. Are we really stuck with using the flip chart or overhead projector?" I responded, "That's true, we will not be able to use the computer this afternoon. I understand that we don't have a new monitor, but you can choose between the flip chart or the overhead projector. Which would you prefer?" I let the group make their own decision or "plan B."

Lessons from Mom: Always Treat People with Respect

As a child, you remember your mother telling you to respect your elders and peers. Regardless of the audiences you encounter, it's imperative to treat them with respect.

Here is an example of an incident that happened to me at a presentation and how I handled it. Many years ago I used to give a discussion entitled "How Nuclear Power Works" to civic groups and various organizations. Nuclear power is not a topic well understood by many people. In fact, some people even fear nuclear power and have a hostile attitude toward it because they do not fully understand it.

I was scheduled to give a thirty-minute lunchtime presentation to a civic organization comprised of many professionals, mostly lawyers. I arrived at the restaurant early to set up for my talk. As I was finishing my preparations, out of nowhere, someone threw an ashtray at me, hitting me over my left eye. In fact, the ashtray cut my eye and I started to bleed. At first I was shocked, but I did not panic. I said to myself, Len, stay professional. You knew they weren't in favor of nuclear power to begin with. You are representing the company; stay professional.

As I picked up a napkin and held it over the cut, I remembered who the audience was. Since I did not see who threw the ashtray, I said with as much grace and confidence as I could muster, "Before I get started, and I know this is not a very popular topic I will be speaking on, but is there a good attorney in the audience?" After I said that, a silence fell over the room. Then I said, "If you promise not to throw any more objects at me, I will begin my speech as I promised, and I hope to answer and address your obvious concerns during my presentation. It is clear to me what some of your views are on this topic. All I ask is that you give me the opportunity to explain mine."

This example illustrates how I combined the strategies of managing a hostile audience, applying the principles of knowing your audience, staying professional, and being respectful.

Confidence Builder: Lessons to Take with You After Your Presentation

Each speech or presentation you give is another opportunity to improve your speaking skills. As a speaker, you can very easily settle into a pattern where everything is familiar and comfortable to you. It's when it is not that you feel the pressure.

In order to grow as a speaker, it is very important to include new material or techniques each time you address an audience. Change your speech by about 10 percent each time you present it, and incorporate new material or techniques. If the new portion fails, so what? You still have 90 percent of your remaining presentation to hold you up. On the other hand, your newer material may go over well with the audience. This is how you develop new material.

Do you ever watch professional comedians on TV? A few of my colleagues are professional comedians, and they always talk about trying out new material on their audience. Sometimes new material does not work the first time. It may be because you didn't practice it enough to give a smooth delivery, or the material may have been wrong for the audience.

Keep a journal of new material you have tried and what worked and failed. Refer to this journal when you are looking to include fresh material into your speech.

Type of Speech: Impromptu Speech

There may be situations when you are called upon to address a group of people with no warning, whether it's in class, work, or social situations.

Here is an example of an impromptu speech as well as a technique I used when asked to present an award at a Boy Scout awards banquet in Connecticut. I had no inclination that I was going to be asked to speak. The scheduled speaker had become ill earlier in the day and was unable to attend. Aware of my background in public speaking, the organization knew I would rise to the challenge. Here's how I prepared for the impromptu speech.

Quickly I found an index card and jotted down notes using the formula TIQS, which is a common formula professional speakers use when they have to introduce a speaker or themselves as the speaker.

- *T* stands for *topic.* What is the actual award and reason for it?
- *I* stands for *importance.* What is significant about this award, and why is it important?
- *Q* stands for *qualifications.* Why is this particular person qualified to receive this award?
- *S* stands for the *subject.* What is the recipient's name?

Since this was a surprise award, I found one of the Scout leaders who was running the awards banquet and asked him these questions. Here are the responses.

- **Topic.** This was the Nutmeg Award, Connecticut is the Nutmeg State, which is given as a spoof annually to an individual who had an event that did not go as planned. The purpose of the award is also to show the boys that it is okay to be lighthearted about your mistakes and that we're all only human. This person, let's call him Jim, was in charge of coordinating a five-mile hike for Boy Scouts, and as part of the drill he had to prepare detailed directions for the boys to go from point A to point B using a compass.

- **Importance.** In scouting we stress the importance of *being prepared,* but in this particular event, one detail was not verified or checked. When Jim wrote down the directions, he inadvertently typed "south" instead of "north" on part of the directions, and as a result about thirty boys got lost. Fortunately, as Scouts they were ready to handle unforeseen obstacles and eventually figured out what was wrong. However, they did not complete the hike in the time allotted.
- **Qualifications.** Jim's qualifications were that he had been doing this for the last fifteen years and had never made any mistakes.
- **Speaker's name.** Jim.

Taking this information, here is the speech I gave.

Boy Scout Nutmeg Award

Ladies, gentlemen, Scout leaders, Scouts, and honored guests. We have one final award to give out this evening, and I have been asked to do the honors. Bill, who was originally scheduled to present this special award, became ill at the last minute and could not be here.

Before I tell you the recipient of this award, let me take a little time to explain what this award is all about. The Nutmeg Award is given every year to one deserving person who, in the eyes of this Scout district, demonstrated initiative and hard work but failed to check all the last minute details. Each year we have the boys go on a short, timed, five-mile hike using di-

rections prepared by one of our leaders and a compass. As many of you know, we have had someone responsible for coordinating this program, and they have done a fine job every year, until this year. You see, for the boys to successfully go from point A to point B as part of this five-mile hike, it is very important for them to follow the directions. Well, they did exactly that, except what they did not know was that the directions had them inadvertently going in the wrong direction. The Scouts realized this about three-quarters of the way into the hike—when they reached a high stone wall, they deduced that something was very wrong. Wisely, a Scout called to one of the leaders, who pointed out that there obviously was some kind of error. Well, the boys found their way back, and the event was rescheduled for a later date.

To honor the person responsible for creating the "clear" directions, I would like to present this year's Nutmeg Award to the person who is most deserving of this award: Jim Healy.

I ask, Jim, that you come up, and while I place this award around your neck, I ask that you wear it proudly as others before you have. You are now a distinguished member of the Nutmeggers Club. Would everyone please give Jim a round of applause?

This speech was a success because I used the TIQS acronym and quickly organized my thoughts and ideas using the mind-mapping technique I discussed in Day 8. The important thing to remember is to find out all the possible facts and details and follow your notes.

Tip of the Day

As a speaker, the most important thing you can do is learn how to truly connect with your audience. The best way to do this is by showing the audience that you are a sincere, real person. People often tell me that they were really impressed that I was willing to share personal stories during my presentations.

In addition, audiences like when a speaker can relate to their problems, issues, or concerns.

In your next presentation have at least one personal story that you can tell your audience to illustrate a point. Whenever possible, especially in the Q&A period, try to relate your answer to what you perceive the person asking the question may be feeling. Demonstrate to your audience that you care about them, and you will be surprised by how much you will improve as a speaker. Finally, remember this quote every time you give a presentation: "No one cares how much you know, unless they know how much you care."

Throughout this book I have talked about the importance of preparation and how you must practice and work continually to improve your speaking abilities. If you follow the tips and concepts I have illustrated, you will become a better and more confident public speaker. If you are like me, you constantly want to work to improve your speaking skills and learn from others. Even as a professional speaker, I am continually learning to hone my craft. Look for one small thing to improve and continue to perform self-evaluations by using a video camera to keep yourself in check. Use audience feedback or evaluation sheets to help guide you to areas that need strengthening.

As you strive to improve, refer often to this book, as it contains sound advice based on many years of experience and what works to help you become a confident public speaker.

About the Authors

The Princeton Language Institute, based in Princeton, New Jersey, is a consortium of language experts, linguists, lexicographers, writers, teachers, and businesspeople that develops easy-to-read self-help books in a nonacademic format for writers, businesspeople, and virtually anyone who wants to enhance his or her communication and language skills. It is the creator of the *21st Century Dictionary of Quotations, 21st Century Grammar Handbook,* and *Roget's 21st Century Thesaurus,* with over one million copies sold.

Lenny Laskowski is an international professional speaker and the president of LJL Seminars based in Newington, Connecticut (www.ljlseminars.com). He is an accomplished public speaker and conducts seminars and workshops at high schools, universities, businesses, and corporations, providing practical techniques that improve one's presentation and communication skills. He is the author of *Dynamic Presentation Skills for the Business Professional.* His work has appeared in various magazines including *Presentations* and *Training.* He resides in Newington, Connecticut.

The Philip Lief Group is a book developer based in Princeton, New Jersey, that produces a wide range of language and usage guides including *Grammar 101, Guide to Pronunciation,* and *Roget's 21st Century Thesaurus.* The Philip Lief Group has been singled out by the *New York Times* for its "consistent bestsellers" and by *Time* magazine for being "bottom-line think tankers."